CONTENTS

Introduction	3
Mia	9
Abbi	38
Lucy	61
Peter	77
Olivia	93
Fliss and Jack	110
Conclusion	140

INTRODUCTION

"This book has been made a reality by my Husband and my Son, along with my Mum, Step-mum and Dad. They, along with my two closest friends in the World; Dawn and Vicky, all made the time to read my book and encourage me to publish it. Thank you x

Most of all though, I dedicate this book to the bravery, determination, kindness and strength shown by not only the young adults I work with but also all of the young adults making their way through life today"

My name is Sarah Terry and I have been working with teenagers for a great deal of my adult working life. It was never something that I set out to do and, I suppose, like most careers, I just fell into it. My first experience of working with teenagers was not as a teacher or any of the other traditional routes that people take, it was my experience of designing and delivering training courses which literally threw me in at the deep end.

My husband owned a leisure facility at the time and had been approached by the local pupil referral unit (PRU) to ask if he could offer some sort of education-based activity for harder to reach teenagers. These were kids who had been thrown out of mainstream school or who had spent time in young offenders' institutions. Unwanted by a school system which couldn't cater for their needs, but still under the mandatory age for leaving education they were statistics, boxes to be ticked. The government had to show that they were still in the care of some type of system and had employed people to see that this happened. There was funding available and money to be made, hence the growth of many local organisations offering solutions to keep these young people off the streets for a few hours a day.

The PRU had asked if my husband would be able to offer some kind of work experience at his facility which had karting, quad bikes, outdoor activities etc. there was also a restaurant on site, which offered another option for a learning activity. My husband had not been keen and was telling me so over a glass of wine one evening.

Whether it was the wine, divine purpose or a moment of madness; I'll never know but I found myself telling him that we could not only offer these young people some practical experiences but we could also build a training course around it where I could teach communication and customer service techniques which was my background and I'd also be able to use my very green counselling skills to "help" them.

The PRU seemed to almost throw money at us and were keen to get things started. Still basking in my self-enhanced glory and congratulating myself on my achievement, I hadn't really stopped to think how this was going to be. Luckily, my naivety worked in my favour. Had I had an inkling of just how demanding the next few years would be, I'd have run a mile.

We got through it, somehow, and bizarrely I enjoyed that time. I don't know why or how but I had a natural affinity with these vulnerable youngsters. Mostly boys, they had been labelled by society as well as their own families and communities. I was not prepared for what they taught me about life, people, humility and prejudice. They were also surprised when their polished one liners and attempts at unravelling me just didn't work. I'd joke along with them but somehow (I don't really know how) I'd maintain enough discipline to get through the day.

The youngsters would start by making themselves and each

other some tea and toast, followed by a team building event which I would try and make as practical as possible. The afternoons were often spent doing practical activities like karting or den building so beforehand, we would have a learning session to suit; e.g. health and safety, racing techniques etc and I would try and get different members of staff to deliver these.

The course became a victim of its own success and thus was somewhat famous locally. The uprising of social media enabled word to spread easily and the PRU were receiving requests to go on the course which created a waiting list. This helped them immensely as they had a bargaining tool with which to establish some order at their facilities.

I won't deny that the positive feedback from the funders, but most importantly, the young people themselves had an effect on me. I felt good in that I was giving something back in a way and getting through to young people who had perhaps never had a positive relationship with another adult in their lives. I was running my own business and working alongside my husband, albeit in very different roles and I was available for my son, himself a teenager navigating his way through secondary school. Life was good.

Then the funding stream was cut.

I spent a few weeks reeling from the news. People who had been calling me regularly would either not take my call or had been re-assigned different roles amidst a massive government re-think. No one seemed to know what was going on and they were all too busy protecting themselves to give me a second thought. I didn't feel this was my vocation in life, I don't really believe in that anyway; but I was struggling with what to do next.

My Clinical Supervisor had told me about a job, counselling teenagers at a school, one day per week. One of her colleagues had been doing the job for some years but was retiring. If I was interested, she would personally recommend me. I took the job and it was a very strange experience. I wasn't a member of staff but also,

I wasn't a guest of the school, therefore I was largely ignored by other members of staff and left to my own devices. Once again, my naivety helped me as I had no expectations and just went with what I thought was the right thing to do. I felt very lonely and like I had failed somehow.

I fumbled my way through the next few months, terrified of saying the wrong thing, terrified of making things worse. Fear gradually gave way to the odd accomplishment and the odd visit from school support staff to share news of students who seemed a little happier. It was from here that my next adventure developed. I was working at several schools and I was finally regarded as a professional in my field.

I had often thought to myself that I should write a book about my experiences. The more I worked with these young people, the more I realised that they had amazing stories to tell and the stories were as inspiring as any modern tale of heroism.

On one very inconsequential day, a girl came to see me. She was a larger than life character who was always in trouble for shouting and disrupting her classes. Her mother had been called into school when it had been discovered that she was self-harming. The girl's mother, herself a larger than life character; was weary and irritated by having to visit the school. She branded her daughter as an attention seeker and told the school to ignore her stupid behaviour and ensure that she got on with the business of learning.

The girl, Anya; was true to her reputation and spent the first ten minutes of our meeting shouting and screaming her woes to me. She was always ignored, never taken seriously, her mother didn't love her, she wanted to live with her Nanna because she sometimes listened to her. Anya then adjusted her sights to her peers. They were all stupid and immature and didn't understand her. No one took her seriously, no one cared. After her initial outburst, Anya stopped dead in her tracks and threw herself back in her chair as she took a sharp intake of breath. She raised her hands to her mouth and with her best look of dramatic shock, she exclaimed, "You're listening to me!" I smiled at her and nodded. "But you *actually* are!" Anya jumped up from her chair and ran over to me, she crouched before me, her hands clutching the sides of her head. "Is that what you do? Listen?"

"Yes, it's one of the things I do Anya"

"Wow!" Anya sat back in her chair and slapped the tops of her thighs in disbelief and joy. "I think I'm going to like you"

Anya was a complicated girl with many issues, some of which were imposed on her but some of which she had embellished. Her mother had been correct when she had branded Anya an attention seeker. Anya was several years older than her 4 siblings and had a different father. She had never met her father and had been told that he wanted nothing to do with her. Anya had been an only child until the age of 9 when her mother met her stepfather. For each of the following 4 years, Anya's mother had given birth to a child. She was busy with her new brood and Anya had been expected to help out, stay quiet and get on with school. When this had not happened, Anya's mother had reacted not with kindness and understanding, but with the irritation of a juggler who had dropped a ball.

Anya, an intelligent and imaginative girl had retreated into the sanctity of her mind and had created a persona which she would ensure would be heard, noticed and perhaps wanted. It helped Anya immensely to be able to rant away and talk of all the silly people who had wronged her and afterwards, she would sit and listen whilst I talked to her about different choices and how they might affect her outcomes. The work was slow, but I knew that Anya got a lot from her time with me.

During one of her sessions, Anya had arrived and told me that she couldn't stay for long as she was in the middle of an IT project which she was rather enjoying and wanted to complete. The project was around the idea of the perfect family and how this could be challenged. Knowing that this would be an ideal opportunity for Anya to reflect and create, I was intrigued to know what she had done.

Anya stood up and prepared her stance as if she were about to conduct a great orchestra.

"You're going to love this! My family has been perfectly created by me. *I'm* the one who has ensured that they are all ok. The scene depicts my children and their children who are all wealthy and drive whatever cars they like. They're not snobby but they can have what they want. They give to charities and look after children who have no parents. They all love each other and stick up for each other and no one can ever come between them. They're happy because I made sure they were happy but I'm not there. I've died. It's in the future, see? So, the scene is me looking down on my family from heaven, but it's ok because I'm happy too. I've done the one and only thing that I wanted to do and now, because I'm dead, I can watch them forever which means I'll be happy forever too." As Anya spoke, she waved her arms and pointed to each of her subjects in turn; seeing them clearly in her mind's eye. As she spoke of herself, she moved across the room and elevated herself onto tipped toes to emulate looking down on her family. "And do you want to know why I'll be especially happy?"

"Of course, I do Anya…"

"Because I'm eating popcorn with Whitney Houston!"

As Anya flounced out of my room, wiping back the tears, I knew would I had to write a book one day.

I'd like to invite you, the reader, to enter my World and the World of these extraordinary young people as I tell you just a few of their stories…

MIA

Mia first came to me when she had moved into year 7 of high school. This would make her 11 years old. She had a social worker who had referred her to me to help her to manage the recent changes that had been forced upon her.

Mia was a little girl with a big personality. Standing no more than shoulder height to my 4'11" she was tiny even for year 7.

Her father being mixed afro Caribbean and her mother white, Mia was mixed race. She sat before me, her milky brown skin and dark brown eyes set within an elfin face almost hidden by a shock of hair falling in ringlets to her waist. The ringlets were partially tamed by a small clip placed on top of her head. Mia sat on her hands, legs swinging as they didn't reach the floor; and she rocked back and forth.

Mia had rather a pronounced tic in her right eye which I found distracting but in a strange way, also made her endearing. Mia rocked back and forth looking at me, her hands still firmly under her legs. She began to grimace in the way a small child would when they are getting angry. Her bottom jaw jutted out and her open lips revealed gritted teeth. Her eyes were now fixed and wide open, staring just past me. Was she about to have some sort of seizure? I felt myself becoming concerned, but I held my position as I felt there was more to come.

Sure enough, after a few seconds, Mia let out a loud, low "Grrrrrrr" and her head began to shake. Mia had now firmly fixed her pretty brown eyes on me and, as I looked, I saw it. Slowly, very slowly and starting at her eyes, Mia began to smile, an almost manic, mischievous smile. What was she trying to tell me? What did she need me to know or do? I held my position still further and the growl began to morph into a low-pitched demonic laugh. Her legs were now swinging in opposing directions and she threw her ringlets back and stared up at the ceiling, looking back at me periodically, I suspect, to check I was still watching her. This went on for about 2 or 3 minutes. The tiny demon in front of me was pulling out all the stops. I sensed she wanted me to intervene or try and stop her, but I didn't, partly because I wanted to observe the behaviour but partly because I was fascinated by it. The more the performance went on, the more I began to like this girl.

When she stopped, Mia looked at me quizzically. Her head was cocked to the side like a puppy. The facial tic returned, the rocking subsided and the hands remained, as they had been all along, under her legs.

"I hate this school, I hate my Dad, and I hate everyone except my Mom! I want my Mom!"

Mia's demeanour changed, her spine curved backwards into a C shape and her face was screwed up like a toddler who had been refused a new toy. She was frowning. I really had been subjected to a full show here.

Finally, I spoke. "Wow" I said. It sounds like you have lots of feelings about lots of things. You say you hate your Dad, and everyone and the school and you want your Mom?"

"I just want my Mom! I hate my Dad!"

"Can I ask where Mom is?"

"I don't know, no one will tell me! They just say I'm not allowed to see her. What do they know? What right do they have to tell me I can't see my own motheeeeeeer?" As Mia finished her sentence, she resumed her demonic grimace and started to growl once again. "Grrrrrrrr I hate them! I HATE them!" She rolled her eyes and sat back in her chair. For the first time, she removed her hands from under her legs and crossed them purposefully in front of her. She gave a huff and flicked her tiny face away from me, staring at the wall...waiting for me to make the next move.

I was happy to oblige. "You seem really angry"

"You would be!"

"Yes, I think if my Mom had disappeared and no one was telling me where she was, I would be angry too."

"I hate this school!"

"Ok..."

"I got sent out of maths just because I moved someone's bag out of the way. I couldn't get past, so I moved this kid's bag and Sir sent me out."

"Really? That sounds like a big reaction from the teacher, just for moving a bag?" I was later to find out that Mia had thrown the bag across the room in a rage.

Mia pushed her hands back under her legs and leaned forward, her legs swinging. The gritted teeth gave way to another growl and this time, her head was shaking with rigid anger. "They're all idiots! Sir! My Dad! Even my Mom! Where is she?"

As I watched Mia, I saw a little girl, scared, alone in the World trying to make sense of her new normal.

"I bet you wouldn't just leave your kid without telling them where you had gone?"

"It's not always that simple. Why don't you tell me a little bit about Mom and when you last saw her?"

"Ages ago" The hands were now in position two, firmly folded in front of her. "And Dad says I'm not allowed to see her or something."

"Ok, so Dad says you're not allowed to see mom. Does Dad say why?"

"Because she's a bad inf.. flu… sense. Something I can't remember the word."

"Influence?"

"Yes, that's it! What does he know? *I* looked after *her* not the other way around!"

Gradually, I began to get an idea of the story. That Mia had somehow been removed from her mother's care and now, for whatever reason, there was no contact.

I work with many young people who have restricted or no access to their parents for a variety of reasons. The pain and suffering caused, not necessarily by the separation itself but by the lack of information given to young people for fear they won't understand or will be sad or angry; can be devastating and can last a lifetime.

In the beginning, Mia was no exception. As far as she was concerned, she had woken up one morning with her life the way it always had been. By the time her confused little head had hit the pillow that night, aged just 10, her life had been taken away, or rather she had been taken away from her life.

"Ok…" I ventured. "So, you say that you don't agree with Dad's reason for you not seeing Mom and that you looked after her? Is your Mom sick?"

"If I tell you, will you have to tell?"

Mia had grown up as no stranger to the social care system. She had been exposed to Social Workers her whole life. To her I was another nosey busy body trying to get information from her to use against her and her family. Well, she was going to show me.

I reminded Mia of the parameters of the confidentiality that can be enjoyed by young people in the school counselling setting. I always explain that, whilst our conversations are confidential, if I have a safeguarding concern, I am obliged to pass this on. I always explain a safeguarding concern to young people as a serious concern about the safety of the student from actions by themselves or others or if their actions pose a safety concern to other people.

"So, if I tell you something, you won't keep it a secret? You'll just blab?"

I repeated the safeguarding information.

"I'm not sure if I should say then."

"Mia. Please be assured that if you are at all worried about yourself or anyone else, we're here to help."

The demonic smile returned. Mia's eyes rolled back in her head like a possessed child and again she gave me the low-pitched laugh which she squeezed the life out of until her face started to turn a reddish purple.

Then within a millisecond, she was sitting, bolt upright with one leg crossed on top of the other. Mia placed her hands daintily on her knee in the fashion of a rather well to do lady. Her back was bolt upright and she was smiling at me. "Well. You see, my mother is not like other mothers." The statement was delivered in a mock aristocratic style of accent. "She's what you might call a druggie you know." Again, she spoke in the mock posh accent.

Many young people will assume another persona when delivering information which they find difficult as a way of removing it slightly from themselves. Mia was no different.

"So, you say your mom takes drugs? Are you comfortable to tell me more?"

"Well you must be pretty stupid if you didn't realise that that was the reason why I don't see her. What else is there to say? They say she can't look after us, but she never did anyway. I did everything and now I'm being treated like a baby! I'm not a baby! I just want to go home."

Apart from the fact that Mia desperately missed her mom, in her mind, there was nothing for her to tell. The rest of it was absolutely normal to her and she couldn't understand why anyone would want to know any more information about her life, let alone why people sought fit to interfere. It would be nearly two years of working together before she would tell me the whole heart breaking and inspiring story.

2

Mia liked to test me and test me she did! Mia would bark inappropriate questions at me, such as "Can I come and live with you?" or "I know who else you see here. What do you talk about?"

Mia would move seamlessly from a young child, scared and alone to a feisty little madam at war with her World.

During one of our sessions, Mia decided that she would test my allegiance to her and told me that she had a secret to tell me which, if I heard it, would mean I had to report it. Once again, I explained the safeguarding procedure in place with the school.

"That means you'll tell" Mia barked at me, she pouted her lips and lifted her chin high, she turned her head away from me very slowly with her eyes purposefully closed. She completed the movement with a flick of her ringlets and came to rest with her arms folded in front of her. The gesture was punctuated with one of Mia's "humphs".

I fixed my gaze on the side of Mia's face waiting for her to turn and face me. The procedure had become almost ritualistic and was a way of her building a way of "being" with me. Mia would spend most of her time moaning about other people, telling me what she would do to them, mostly she would want to "kick them in the face" and each week, there was an ever-increasing list of people whom Mia hated and deserved to be kicked in the face. I would listen patiently to the list, questioning the reason for each and then supporting Mia to look at things differently, for what it was worth.

Mia opened her eyes and looked around at me without moving her head. As she met my gaze, we both burst into uncontrollable laughter. The few moments that we shared laughing, each of us knowing exactly why we were laughing was, I felt, a turning point for our relationship. Mia had tried everything to make me shocked, angry, dismissive and none of it had worked. She had truly used all her bag of tricks and now, faced with my constant return and my refusal to dismiss her I was starting to feel that we may be opening the door to some real quality work together. As Mia was about to show me, however, I couldn't have been further from the truth.

As our laughter subsided, and we both began to compose ourselves, Mia asked again if she could tell me her secret. I reminded her once again of the safeguarding procedure and that if I felt she was in immediate danger, I would, indeed have to report the matter. After some more discussion, I began to feel that Mia really wanted to tell me something. I tried to reassure her that there would be full discussion before I reported anything. Eventually, Mia began to speak.

"Well..." she was perched on the edge of her chair with her legs crossed and her clasped hands placed on her knees. This adult demeanour brought to mind a teacher talking to a student. What was Mia "teaching" me? "Last night.....right?"

"Yes"

"Well, last night…I did something really bad" Mia was rocking from side to side, maintaining her pose but the eye contact had gone. As Mia casually flicked several shiny black ringlets back over her shoulder, her eyes were deliberately, anywhere but meeting mine.

"Ok, so last night, you did something?"

"Yes. And the thing that I did is really bad and if people find out they'll take me away from my Dad's and Social Services will come and it'll all be really bad." As Mia acted her way through the words, I felt in my gut that there was something amiss, but I stayed present with Mia because she was telling me, teaching me something else.

"Ok, so you did something that you think will bring some bad consequences for you or dad?"

"Yup"

"Sometimes, we can really worry that something will cause a lot of trouble but actually it can be sorted out. You're doing really well."

"Well, I went downstairs when Dad wasn't looking, and I got hold of some washing line. I took the washing line up to my room and tied it around my neck. Then I tied it to the light fixing. I jumped off my bed, but the line was too long, and nothing happened." The disclosure was delivered in an uncharacteristically monotone voice and in a very adult, calm and, dare I say, rehearsed way.

Nevertheless, my first duty is to the safety of the child and I clearly had to report this disclosure, despite my thoughts surrounding it. I was also keen to see how Mia would react when I told her that I would have to report what she had told me.

"Ok, well, I think you know…" Before I could finish the sentence, Mia was begging me not to tell.

"Please, please don't tell anyone, please! I'll say you are lying and that you made it up! I'll deny it! If you say anything, I'll NEVER speak to you EVER again!" The dramatic gestures and childlike demands had returned. In my heart, I knew that this was a test. I knew that Mia wanted me to keep this most dangerous of disclosures between us and that this would prove that she could trust me beyond anyone else never to tell. I also knew in this moment that Mia wanted to make a connection with me that she could hold inside herself and feel safe that no one could penetrate it. I knew exactly what Mia wanted and I knew that I was breaking her heart.

Much like a detective interviewing a criminal, a good counsellor develops a sixth sense for the truth and is able to see beyond the words being spoken. Even though counselling is about believing the client, it is more often than not, about looking beyond what we are being told, the context we are being told in and the stage in the counselling relationship at which a disclosure is made. With Mia I had seen what was going on and I was 99% sure it was about her and me.

In counselling, one of the first and most important skills to be learned and one which requires constant attention is that of effective boundary setting. This can be especially hard when working with young people who, far from understanding the premise of counselling, naturally want to get close to an adult who treats them with respect and takes time to listen to them. Mia wanted to cross this boundary and change our relationship to bring us closer together.

I knew that in Mia's mind, I was seriously damaging our relationship but there was no question of me not reporting the disclosure, even if it meant she would not see me again. Mia was now on the floor at my feet begging me not to tell, she told me that she had made the whole thing up just to see what I would do. This I believed.

"I'm sorry that you are upset but I would not be keeping you safe if I didn't pass this information on"

"But what will happen? Will they call my Dad?" There was desperation in Mia's voice. Her tic was now very prominent, her right eye and the right side of her face twitching uncontrollably.

"Yes. They will call Dad, they have to."

Mia sat back on her bottom, still on the floor, she looked dejected. She crossed her legs and played with her fingers, her head bowed, like a toddler.

"Would you like me to tell you what happens next?" I ventured.

"No. I hate you!" Mia stood up and flounced out of the room, slamming the door behind her. I suspect at that moment, she really wanted to kick me in the face.

3

The next few weeks consisted of Mia ensuring that she was in the school reception when I arrived. Whilst ignoring me in the most dramatic way she could, Mia would ask loudly, "Am I down to see Sarah today?" Each time the receptionist would glance at me before checking my list. I would stand quietly whilst Mia was told that, yes; she was listed to see me today. "Well can you tell her that I won't see her, and tell her not to come to collect me from class as I will not go with her?" I would make no reaction and would add Mia to the following week's list.

During a catch-up with student support staff, the subject of Mia had been discussed. Mia had made sure that everyone she had been in contact with had known that I had betrayed her and that I had been added to her now gargantuan list of "hatees". On the lighter side, however, in her attempt to ignore me, she was getting into school early every Wednesday and staying in all of her lessons to avoid me. Mia was far from stupid, as she had demonstrated on many occasions and I knew that one day we would work together again, I just had to accept my "punishment".

That came some months later. Mia had now moved into Year 8 of Secondary School and things hadn't seemed to have changed at all for her. She had befriended some girls in Year 11. These girls were just as troubled and confused as Mia, all sharing the common traits of behavioural problems, absenteeism, academic failings. As humans, we have an uncanny ability to sniff out our "pack". They give off micro signals which can be read if we have a commonality. Sometimes this can be a supportive and protective environment but often, these packs will consist of a maelstrom of emotion with no apparent "leader" and no ability to form and maintain hierarchical relationships. This is a pack made up of needy children, all seeking to protect the needy child they see in each other but the almighty clash between what they want and what they are emotionally capable of creates negative energy so powerful that the Hadron collider, the enormous vessel designed to split the atom; lies in its wake.

This particular group was no different. It consisted mostly of girls who saw themselves in Mia and wanted to somehow rewrite her future, thus rewriting their own. In their efforts to change Mia, they would gradually relive and revisit their own tragic lives and the initial desire to help her, mixed with Mia's own inability to cope emotionally with this new-found attention; rapidly transformed into her being ostracised from the group.

I was called to the student support office where Mia was sitting, crying but trying desperately not to show it. As I entered, she scowled at me. All I saw was that scared little girl wearing a mask of protection which was as transparent to me as it was to all around her.

"Hi Mia, long time no see. How are you?" I greeted Mia as openly as I could, hoping that she would not feel backed into a corner of her own making and hoping that she would not refuse to speak to me out of her own embarrassment. As I smiled at Mia, her scowl faded a little as she sniffed a tear away.

"Mia has had a few problems in the last week or so." the student support officer interjected. "She has fallen out with her friends and is feeling a bit lonely". Mia sat silently whilst the support officer continued. "We thought that it might help Mia to have someone to talk to about how she is feeling, and Mia has agreed to talk to you".

"Ok, that sounds great. Mia when do you want to see me? I can make time today if you like?" Mia sniffed again and with the tiniest nod of her head affirmed that this would be ok.

Later that day, I sent for Mia and she dutifully came to my room. Still sullen, she had her coat in her arms. Mia sat down and placed her coat over the front of her body. She pulled the hood of the coat up around her face and nuzzled her hands inside the hood to hold it in place. Mia sat for a while, blinking slowly. She was still tiny; her body was more like an 8-year-old. The first thing I noticed was Mia's hair. The black shiny ringlets had been brutally straightened and the straight black hair had been strategically placed to cover what looked like patches of hair which could only have been an inch long. I could tell that Mia was clearly self-conscious about her hair, but I had also seen a similar occurrence before in a mixed-race girl that I worked with. She would straighten her hair and cut chunks away so that it looked thinner somehow. I wondered if Mia had done the same, but I decided not to mention the hair right now.

Mia sat lazily on her chair, her bottom pushed forward and her head as far back as possible. Her tiny legs were stretched out in front of her in a rather boyish defiant manner. Her feet waggled and she sighed as if she were bored. I studied Mia for a few moments, it was clear that she had been spending time with older students, she had accurately mimicked the laissez faire body language and the eminent mixture of "don't speak to me" and "I can't be bothered". Mia stared out of the window, her jacket hood brushing along her lips hiding as much of her face as possible.

"So, Mia, what happened? Mrs. Stokes said that you have fallen out with your friends?"

Mia shrugged; this was the only physical movement she gave.

"Have you been friends a long time?" Another shrug.

"I can see that you're a little upset at the moment". This time the shrug was accompanied by a fidgety re adjustment in her chair. As I looked at Mia's eyes, still firmly fixed on the window, I saw that they were full of tears. Before the tears could roll down her face, Mia sniffed vigorously and simultaneously wiped her face with her hood, hoping I'm sure, that I hadn't noticed.

"You're upset?" I ventured. This time the shrug was accompanied by a sarcastic raise of the eyebrows. It was as if she had said to me, "Of course I'm bloody upset! What a stupid question!"

One of the many challenges of working as a school counsellor is the lack of time. As Mia had been a last-minute addition to my day, I had little time to spend with her. I had to move things along without her feeling that I was dismissing her. I explained that I hadn't set aside a time allotment for her that day, but would she like to come and see me next week? Mia gave a shrug of acknowledgment and I told her that I would look forward to seeing her next week, but I had to finish now as there was another student waiting to see me. As I stood and moved to the door, Mia sat still for a few seconds and then slowly began to gather her bags, still trying to hold her coat around her face.

"It's been great to see you today Mia. We'll have more time next week".

In what seemed like one and the same movement, Mia dropped her bag and her coat and threw her arms around my waist, burying her face into my chest. My natural reaction was to return the hug although I felt extremely awkward and exposed. I placed my hands-on Mia's arms and she intensified her grip on my waist. Within seconds, it was over, and Mia had gone, not speaking or making eye contact once.

I stood for a while, still in the same pose, my arms outstretched and curled in front of me; as if it were possible to bring Mia back into the room and place her where she had been with her tiny frame pushed against me, clinging to me as if her life depended on it. This had been a pure, raw expression of emotion from Mia who had been holding fear, anger, resentment and confusion inside of her for most of her life. I hoped that Mia had gotten some comfort from the hug. I imagined how desperate she must be for someone to put their arms around her and tell her she was ok and how desperately she must have wanted to melt into my arms and feel safe and secure even though I suspected she didn't even know what that meant.

As I began to regroup and think about what had just happened, I noticed a single tear roll down my cheek. Before I had time to notice what I was doing, I was clumsily wiping the tear away with my sleeve. I couldn't stop thinking about how I had wanted to hug Mia tightly and tell her that everything was going to be ok. Just as she had transferred her anguish to me via our physical contact, I wanted to swap it and send her a virtual infusion of strength and comfort.

It is perhaps in these moments that I feel most helpless. I can easily feel as though, far from helping these young adults, I'm exacerbating their pain by offering them a glimpse of a relationship which can never last. It is at these times that I wonder why I feel the need to do this job and whether I even have the right.

Before I saw Mia the following week, I spent a lot of time reflecting on the hug and my feelings about it. I had numerous internal wrangles. Should I discuss it? Should I explain that it wasn't appropriate? I imagined what the Senior Management Team at the school would say. They would possibly even view it as a safeguarding incident and stop me from working with Mia. I had decided that I could handle things and I chose to talk to my clinical supervisor about the incident.

As I am self-employed, I pay privately to meet with a clinical supervisor every month to discuss my work. Clinical supervision is where a psychotherapy professional talks to another psychotherapy professional about their caseload. The meetings tend to be fairly formal in nature and must not be confused with a counselling session, even though clinical supervisors are often counsellors. I am extremely lucky to have found a very experienced counsellor who also used to work as a teacher and has been a school counsellor. Now a Senior Accredited Supervisor for the British Association of Counselling and Psychotherapy, she helps me talk through any issues which might bother me and advises me on continuing professional development, safeguarding, etc. Most importantly, she understands the feelings that working with young people can bring up for the counsellor and for the young person.

She pointed out, as I knew she would, that there was clearly something going on here for me for it to have affected me so deeply. I have dealt with young people falling in a motherly sort of love with me before and I understand how easily this can happen. I usually use the feelings to help the young person to understand that they are capable of feeling love and compassion for themselves and others.

"Were you ever in need of a hug when you were little?"

Bang!

I began to fidget on the sofa in my supervisor's cosy consulting room, which now didn't feel so cosy. She sat, motionless waiting for me to compute what she had just said.

As I explained earlier, supervision is not a counselling session for the therapist but occasionally, because we are human, feelings get confused and our own memories can get in the way of our work.

I sat and thought for a while until I realised that I had a very clear memory of my Dad sitting on our sofa at home cuddling my younger sister. She was in her pyjamas as was I. We must have been bathed and ready for bed. I would have been around 6 and my sister, 4. Having Dad at home in the evenings was fairly rare. I was sitting on the opposite chair, scowling at them (much like Mia's scowl) and thinking how disgusting it was that they were cuddling.

I told my supervisor that I had been a "difficult" child or so was the narrative of my younger years. This was in direct opposition to the "easy" child, my sister. I "didn't like affection" and would fidget away from the arms of my Dad often.

As I know, with siblings, each will take on a role that they can call their own, naughty, funny, clumsy, or in our case, easy and difficult. I also know that this was the case with me and my sister and have worked through this many times. This incident with Mia however, had opened the book of my life once again only this time at a page which I was not expecting.

"So, there you were, sitting on the chair, thinking how disgusting it was that your Dad and your sister were cuddling. Were there any times when you would have liked that to be you?"

I started to cry. My supervisor reached for her box of tissues and offered them to me as I had done so many times with my clients.

"This is silly." I said. "I'm not even that upset about it."

"Then why are you crying?"

"I don't know."

"Who is crying?" I knew exactly what she meant. It wasn't the "me" of the here and now that was crying. It was the 6-year-old me, the child who had learned to replace her tears so well with that scowl, just like Mia. It was the 6-year-old that needed a hug to make everything alright. Because of her reputation though, she could not be seen to ask for or even respond to a hug. Instead she had to look on whilst her sister got what she so desperately wanted.

When Mia had hugged me, when she had opened her heart for a brief moment, she had forgotten to scowl or to hate, her primeval instincts had taken over and she had sought love and protection from someone whom she thought could give it. And in that moment, I hadn't been hugging Mia at all. It wasn't Mia I wanted to save; it was me.

Once I had processed this in my mind, I was able to see it for the human moment that it was, and my faith in myself and in my work, had been restored. Just as well, as it was time to see Mia.

Mia came bounding into my room and threw herself onto the chair. She was beaming. Mia adjusted herself in the chair, legs swinging, leaning slightly forward with her hands in her lap. Mia smiled at me, her tic twitching as she did so. Mia looked up at the ceiling, still smiling. Her face began to scrunch up starting with her eyes until the whole of her tiny face was wrinkled up. After a short while, a grimace began to form in the corners of Mia's mouth. Her teeth were now visible, and she sat on her hands as her body began to rock in her chair. Stifling a smile, she began to speak. "Grrrrrrrrrrrr. Oh, my Gooooooooddd, I really wanna kick Mr Smith in the face!"

4

I continued to see Mia for the rest of Year 8, and she seemed to improve slightly. Mia had a very good relationship with most of her teachers but struggled with her peers who saw her as controlling and manipulative. Teachers had noticed that if they gave Mia a job to do and involved her in some way as an assistant, she responded very well. It was almost as if Mia didn't see herself as a student but as another adult which is what she believed she was.

Unfortunately, however, Mia was not able to conduct herself in a responsible way with her classmates who also were not able to understand why Mia felt the need to test them and push them away to see if they came back.

When Mia returned to me in Year 9 once again, she had barely changed physically. The makeup she had started to apply looked almost garish and reminded me of a small child competing in a beauty pageant. Many of the girls Mia's age were starting to change shape and look more like young women. Mia would complain to me that she hated herself and wanted boobs and a bum. It had been reported to me that she had posted a picture of herself on Instagram in some hot pants and had been berated by most of her year group for looking like a boy.

I felt the lack of a female role model in Mia's life and saw that she was struggling with herself and her own image. Mia was beginning to notice herself physically and the pain of not being an adult stared back at her in the mirror.

Mia was still frequenting with older children outside of school and most of them were not the sort of people that most parents would want their 13-year-old daughter to be with. Mia's lack of motherly input was impacting on her behaviour more and more.

Mia now had a better relationship with her father but still longed to see her mother whom she saw intermittently. I knew that Mia was yearning for the affection that she needed. Her father was loving but tended to treat her like a little sister rather than a daughter. He would lavish gifts on Mia, and they would play fight and then go and cook tea together. All of these stories were happy ones but there was a gaping hole where I felt a maternal influence would have made all the difference. Over our time working together, I would sometimes fulfil this role for Mia who would ask advice on boys, tell me about snap chat stories and ask me about my own son, asking me if I would let him do this or that.

I sometimes used this to my advantage such as the time Mia

flounced into my room sporting an enormous love bite on her neck. I sighed in horror whilst staring at Mia's neck. "What is THAT Mia?"

"What does it look like? Doh" Mia teased.

"It's gross Mia"

"Don't you like them?"

"No. They're horrible it's like being branded!" I blurted.

Mia touched her neck with her hand and pulled her school shirt around tightly so that I could no longer see the love bite. "If I was your daughter, would you tell me off?" Mia was grinning at me and I knew that my opinion mattered to her, so I saw an opportunity to work with this.

"Yes, I most certainly would! You are a beautiful girl and you don't need to be walking around with bruises on your neck. If he wants everyone to know you're his girl, let him buy you a necklace instead of trying to make one with his mouth!"

We giggled together but I knew that Mia had listened and understood. I never saw her with a love bite again and I had also heard through the school grapevine that she had told another girl who had a love bite that it was gross and she should tell her boyfriend to eat before he saw her!

Things seemed to improve for a while with Mia. She was attending school steadily and was making new friends. Mia had been seeing her mom more often under the supervision of her dad and this seemed to be helping to settle her. Mom had even been around for tea and was due to come for Christmas day with Mia, her Dad and his family.

Not long after we returned to school following the Christmas break, Mia was hovering outside of my door staring into my room through the small strip of glass in the door.

I tend to sit facing the door and students generally sit on the wall which hosts the door which helps them to not be seen.

I waited until there was an appropriate moment with the student I was seeing, and I went outside to Mia. She looked like her World had caved in.

"Are you ok Mia? Your appointment is after lunch, were you here to check?" Mia gave no reaction except to look at me with the desperation of a puppy starved of attention. Her mouth was down turned and her eyes full of tears. She was shuffling from one foot to another. Her face said she was desperate to talk but no words would come.

"Can you see me before?" she managed to mutter.

"I'm sorry no I can't. I'm full until our appointment" Mia turned around slowly and made her way down the corridor, her head bowed and her arms motionless by her side. I wondered what could have happened.

I usually stay in my room for a proportion of lunchtime and I tell students who have recently stopped seeing me that they can come in for drop in sessions if they wish to catch up. Mia arrived 10 minutes before the end of lunch break and stood outside my door gazing in. I motioned her to come in and she entered slowly, standing in the middle of the room. "Are you ok?" I asked, gesturing Mia to sit.

Mia shook her head slowly.

"What's happened?"

After a few seconds, Mia announced, "I HATE my mom!"

Well this was certainly a first. Mia had always protected her mom and had defended her even when she had told me that her mom was in prison for dealing drugs and neglecting Mia and her brothers.

"Ok, so what happened with mom then? This is unusual for you?"

"She told my Dad she wished she never had me" Mia delivered the statement with a childish pout and crossed her arms to complete her sentence. "Well *I* wish she never had me too! I hate her!"

"OK so tell me more, you say that Dad told you she wishes she never had you?"

"No, Dad didn't tell me, she told Dad and I heard her! They were in the kitchen and she said that her life would have been much easier if she never had kids"

My mind was racing. I was torn between my own thoughts about Mia's mother and her continuing behaviour and Mia's adoration for her. I knew that this would break Mia and could have catastrophic consequences.

"Ok" I ventured, "Let's think about why Mom may have said that. Can you remember the conversation leading up to it and maybe after she said it?"

"They were washing up after tea and she was moaning about having to visit all of us individually instead of seeing us all at once. Dad said something about that being her own fault and then she said it."

"Ok, so maybe she meant that her life was really difficult at the moment and she perhaps doesn't feel like things are natural between her and you and your brothers? Did you ask her about it?"

"No. Why should I? If that's what she thinks I can't change anything. Maybe she should think about all the things I did for her and my brothers when we lived at home. Her life was never difficult 'cuz I made sure it wasn't"

I was beginning to see the bigger picture here and I suddenly realised that this was about much more than a throw away comment. This had brought up feelings for Mia which she struggled to comprehend. How was it that her mother could complain about being a mother when in Mia's eyes she never had been? In fact, Mia had seen herself as the mother. It dawned on me that my assumption that Mia was upset and feeling unwanted was misplaced. Mia was in fact angry that her mother could find it difficult to do a job that she herself had done and she must also have felt that, at times, at many times, that her life would be easier if she didn't have children.

It felt like the right time to ask Mia about her home life, she had barely ever mentioned it before, but the opportunity seemed to be presenting itself, so I seized the moment.

"Mia, tell me about when you lived with your mom." I leaned towards Mia and engaged her eyes solidly with mine. I smiled and leaned back again in my chair.

"I've already told you!" Mia scowled.

"You've never really talked about it. You told me that you looked after your two younger brothers a lot but that's all I really know."

"I used to have to feed them, get them up, change them, do the washing, and do the shopping. Everything!"

"Wow so I can see how difficult it must have been when you went to live with Dad and became a child in the home."

Mia fidgeted a little in her chair to make herself more comfortable and began her story. "I was 9 years old when HE moved in. My mom was brilliant before she met him it was all HIS fault. She was really good at saving money; she had a job and we went on holidays. In an aeroplane. Abroad and everything"

"Wow that must have been really exciting?"

"Yes, we went with my Nan and me and my two brothers it was ace."

"So how old were you when you went on holiday?"

"I was 7 the first time and 8 the second time"

"So, life sounds pretty good so far, what happened next?"

Mia shifted in her chair again. Her face changed from a wistful child remembering happy times to the scowl I had come to know so well. "HE came."

Mia went on to tell me that her mother had met her stepfather and very quickly he had moved in and things changed. Mia's mother would often be drunk with him and unable to prepare the family meal. He would become aggressive when Mia's brothers cried for their tea, so Mia took over to keep things quiet. Mia's apparent ability to look after her brothers meant that her mother could not only spend more time drunk but would also go out a lot, leaving Mia to put her brothers to bed and herself.

As time went on, Mia's mother would become increasingly distant and Mia noticed that she would be under the control of her stepfather more and more. It now seemed to be him that decided what happened in the home. Mia had never liked him and had not hesitated to show her feelings. In the beginning he tried to win her over with gifts and bribes. Once he had realised that this did not work, he started to verbally abuse Mia. She would become known as "The Nigger" and would always be referred to as such by him, except on the rare occasion they were in public as a family. Mia's stepfather rarely addressed her directly, he would give his orders via Mia's mother, "Tell the Nigger we're out tonight. She'll have to feed herself and the boys." Far from defending her daughter, Mia's mother would dutifully relay the instruction to Mia.

The abuse started gradually and was so subtle it could almost have been mistaken for accidents. There were times when he would knock Mia's drink over whilst no one was looking. "Look what you've done Nigger! Clean it up you useless Twat!" Mia would often look to her mother for support, but it never came.

Another time, he walked across the room and barged into Mia, knocking her to the floor. "Look at ya, ya can't even walk properly, p'raps ya should crawl around like a monkey. Ha let's face it; we wouldn't know the difference!"

During this time, Mia's stepfather's "friends" became more and more frequent visitors. They would often be at Mia's home when she arrived from school and would still be there when Mia had taken herself and her brothers to bed. The children's' instructions were to keep out of the way except when Mia was sometimes ordered to make tea and coffee for them. Mia had not realised what was going on at this time, but she did know that it was bad. There were various bits and pieces of drug paraphernalia around the place which Mia tried to keep away from her brothers as much as she could. Mia would try desperately to keep a low profile when they were "sleeping" and move syringes, foil and butt ends from the lounge and kitchen. One time, one of them woke up and grabbed Mia's leg as she passed him lying on the lounge floor. "What ya doing Nigger?" He slurred. Mia's tummy flipped as she stood still, frozen to the spot, praying that HE didn't notice. "Coz if ya's nickin me gear I'll fuckin make ya pay. And since ya 'avent got any money, I'll 'av to think of a better way." As he spoke, Mia looked down at him as a grin spread across his face and his hand gradually worked its way up Mia's leg past the point of her school skirt. Before Mia knew it, her fear turned to rage. She yanked her leg from his grip.

"What happened Mia?" I was engrossed in her story and desperately wanted to know what our heroine did next.

With a look of sheer determination, and with a smile starting to spread into the corners of her mouth, she announced, "I kicked him in the face!"

For a moment we just stared at each other. I wasn't sure how to react, but this tense and terrifying moment had been underlined with a bittersweet comedic irony. Mia's over used threat of violence had actually been the way in which she had defended herself against the advances of someone whom she had every right to hate.

Mia's smile faded as she continued. "He deserved it but guess who woke up?" I was immediately gripped once again by Mia's story. My admiration for her courage and resilience was growing more and more and I felt at this moment like a useless spectator hooked on my desire to hear the end of the tale.

Mia told me how he had awoken to the cries of his friend who was nursing the beginnings of a black eye. "What the fuck 'ave you done you useless Nigger?" He pushed Mia's mother from his chest as they lay on the sofa. She groaned as she readjusted herself and returned to her stupor. Mia was willing her to wake up, but she didn't.

"Right you fuckin' little whore, get 'ere. I've been waitin' to sort you out for eva ya Black bitch!"

Mia ran into the kitchen and shut the door behind her. She desperately looked for somewhere to hide but there was nowhere to go. She could have exited the house via the back door but that would have meant that she left her brothers behind. Mia crouched down under the kitchen table. He burst into the room "Get 'ere!" He walked around the room and suddenly his grey sullen face appeared under the table. "Ya can't even fuckin' hide properly!" He reached under the table and pulled Mia out by her arm. His vice-like grip felt like a thousand bees stinging her all at once.

By now there was a lot of commotion coming from the lounge and Mia could hear voices approaching. The kitchen door opened and in came Mia's mother with a couple of men. "Come on love, she ay worth it. If ya hit 'er the fuckin' Social 'll be all over us and that'll be the end for ya business." Whether Mia's mother had said these words in truth or to protect her daughter, Mia didn't care, she just hoped he listened.

"Yeh, come on Col, forget the little shit" Added one of the men.

He looked at them and looked at Mia, his grip still as strong. After what seemed like several minutes, he threw Mia to the ground. "Well ya's stayin' in 'ere. I don't wanna see yer ugly nigger face again! Gorrit?" Mia nodded as she nursed her already bruised arm. "Get the lads as well, she may as well cook 'em their tea while she's in 'ere"

After a few seconds, Mia's brothers came running into the kitchen and hugged her. They had been terrified by the shouting and were glad to be in the safe arms of their sister again. Mia stood up and moved towards the kitchen door to close it. Before she could grab the door, he had already got hold of it. The other adults had left, it was just Him, Mia and the boys. Mia's hand was on the door frame. He held it in place by her wrist. With his eyes fully fixed on hers, he slammed the door, trapping her fingers on the frame. It took a few seconds for the pain to register but she knew it was coming. Her fingers were burning and throbbing, and she was in excruciating pain, but she stared back, defiantly, her eyes full of hate and pain. He opened the door and did it again, all the time holding her gaze. Mia made no sound or reaction except for the tears rolling down her cheeks. He slammed the door on her fingers 3 times in total before throwing her to the ground once more. He turned to Mia as she lay on the ground holding her hand and spat on her. It was at this moment that she decided to tell.

Mia knew that things had changed and that it would only be a matter of time before the beatings would become more often and more intense. She knew she was strong enough to deal with him, but her brothers were not. Mia got up for school the next morning. It took a few seconds for her body to register the pain in her fingers as she looked down at her hand, she noticed that the nail on her middle finger was missing and her fingers were black and blue and covered in blood. Mia found a flannel in the bathroom and ran it under the cold tap until it was wet through. She wrapped the flannel around her finger and continued to get her brothers ready for school. Mia went into her mother's bedroom and took £3 from her purse. On the way to school, she bought lunch for her brothers and a chocolate bar for herself.

Mia had decided that she would tell one of her dinner ladies about what had happened. She was a kind lady and always gave Mia a little extra food when she could afford a school dinner. Mia had also seen her outside of school with her own children and had decided that she was a good mom and would care.

Mia didn't make it to lunchtime however, the pain in her fingers had become so bad that she felt sick and had to ask to go to the toilet. The next thing Mia remembered was lying in the school medical room with several teachers around her. She groaned and tried to sit up. "No, come on Mia, stay where you are sweetheart" Mia's instinct was to get away; she felt trapped and began to cry out. "Let me go!"

The teachers backed away from Mia's bed, sensing that she felt threatened. "Mia, we've got you a drink and a sandwich here, can you eat anything?" Mia shook her head and as she did so, she felt nauseous again. Mia flopped back onto the bed. She could hear voices in the background. "Yes, we've called Mum, no answer but we left a message"

"Have Social Services been notified?"

"Yes, they are sending a police officer and will be here soon. Poor little thing, look at the state of her"

It was at this point that circumstances overtook Mia. The police arrived and went with Mia to the local hospital where she received medical attention and some pain relief. Mia was desperate to know where her brothers were. "They're safe Mia, they're at school and one of my colleagues is with them"

"Don't...please don't let them go home! He'll kill them!" by now Mia was delirious with the pain and the shock of the situation but she knew she had to make sure her brothers were safe.

"Ok Mia, we can see that something has happened here. Can you tell me how you got the bruises on your arm and how you hurt your hand?" Mia's cries subsided and she looked at the police officer. He looked very large and wore a bright yellow jacket which rustled a lot when he moved. He had a radio on his shoulder that kept beeping and every so often, he would talk into it. He looked big enough to protect Mia and her brothers and she decided that he could help her.

"HIM! He's evil and he's horrible to my Mom and last night he did this to me, he slammed my fingers in the door!" Almost as soon as Mia finished talking to the policeman, he put his hand out to her in a reassuring manner, told her everything was going to be ok and stood up and left the room whilst talking into his radio.

Mia had thought that this would be an end to the misery they had all been through. The big policeman would go to her house and take Him away so that Mia, her brothers and her mom would all go back to how they were.

"Humph! And guess what? They took my Mom AND my brothers, and I had to go and live with my stupid Dad! I HATE my life"

As I gradually returned to the room after being in the midst of Mia's story, I gathered my thoughts. Mia sat silently in front of me, her face twitching, waiting for me to say something.

"Mia, your story is really terrifying, you must have felt so alone but your strength is amazing, and you were strong not just for yourself but for your brothers too"

"I've never told anyone what I've just told you. My Mom told me that I could never tell anyone, so I didn't."

"And how do you feel now that you've told your story?"

"It's weird. It feels like I'm talking about someone else"

"And what would you want to say to that person if they just told you that story?"

"Dunno. Maybe that I felt a bit sorry for them?"

"So, do you feel sorry for yourself that you had to go through that?"

"No."

"What do you feel?"

"Maybe a bit better for saying it out loud? You know, I would never have told anyone but you what I've just said"

"Well I feel truly honoured that you chose me to hear your story Mia"

"Honoured? You Saddo!" We shared a grin with each other, and Mia got up to leave my room and return to her lesson. As she got to the door, she turned and rustled in her pocket. Mia pulled out a mint humbug and put it down on my table. "That's my last mint. I want you to have it"

"Thank you, Mia, see you next week"

ABBI

I felt nervous waiting for Abbi to see me that first day. She had been referred as an emergency by the school who had cancelled one of my regular young people to make space for me to see her. I had been called into the Inclusion Manager's office and told that Abbi had suffered some sort of breakdown at school and they and her Foster parents were at their wits' end. There was involvement from Social Services and the Child and Adolescent Mental Health Service (CAMHS) which so far did not seem to be helping.

Jean, the Inclusion Manager looked at me desperately. She was a deeply caring woman, sometimes too caring. She had been beaten down by years of managing teenagers, their parents and their teachers. What Jean *did* have, however, was an amazing sixth sense and if she suspected that something wasn't quite adding up with a story, I had very quickly learned to sit up and listen.

"There's just something not quite right here." Jean had explained. "Abbi is very openly gay and wants to have transgender reassignment to become a boy. Her Foster mother is dead against it and won't even entertain the idea. CAMHS have interviewed Abbi and say because she is 16, she is too young to know either way. It's just a mess and it feels wrong. I'm really hoping you can work your magic here and get to the bottom of it…please?"

No pressure then! So, Social services and the NHS had failed; along with the school and the foster parents to get anywhere with this girl? Oh, and by the way, she wants to be a boy! Magic was indeed what I needed.

As Abbi entered the waiting room, I heard Jean go through to meet her. "You'll really like Sarah; she's down to earth and a bit bonkers so she fits in really well with us." By the time they reached my room, Abbi had a nervous smile on her face.

"Hello Abbi, I'm Sarah. It's a pleasure to meet you. Are you happy for Jean to leave us to chat?" Abbi nodded her head and turned to Jean for reassurance. Jean laid her hands-on Abbi's shoulders and gave them a squeeze. "You'll be safe with Sarah, Love" Abbi turned around in an almost robotic manner and walked over to the chair. Her waist long, sandy hair fell in front of her face and she used this to full effect to mask her face from me.

Abbi sat down and I was distracted by the length of her slender legs. They seemed so long that she barely knew how to contain them. I thought of a baby giraffe trying to stand and manoeuvre itself for the first time. Eventually her legs were brought to rest crossed in front of her and out to one side she tugged her school skirt down her thighs and picked at her black woollen tights with her head still down. "Abbi, I just want to add to what Jean told you. Everything we talk about is confidential, so I want you to speak freely when you feel able to do so. The only time I would have to share anything that you told me was if there was a safeguarding issue, which means, you were in danger or someone else was in danger. Do you understand?" Abbi nodded her bowed head.

Usually when I meet a student for the first time, I talk about what they might come to expect from counselling but I felt the urgency of this situation and felt that it would be more helpful to hear from Abbi whether she thought this would be a good idea or not so I decided to get straight to the point. "Jean tells me you've been having a rough time of it lately"

It was as if I had flicked the "on" switch and Abbi came to life. She raised her head and within the same movement shook her hair from side to side. As her shimmering sandy mane moved from side to side, Abbi used her hands to push it behind her shoulders. This revealed her long slender neck and her square jaw all covered in an English rose complexion any supermodel would envy. I couldn't help but think to myself what a beautiful woman she would become and what a shame it was that she hated this vision that stared back at her in the mirror. My thoughts were duly thwarted and sent to the depths of my mind for me to ponder later.

Abbi picked at the knees of her tights whilst the words were forming. Her pale complexion began to change. Her neck became blotchy and this spread to her face. As it reached her eyes, they also became bloodshot as tears formed. Abbi sniffed her tears away and wiped her eyes with her index fingers. I offered her a tissue which she took, and she dabbed at her eyes. "Grrrr! I didn't want to bloody cry!" I stayed silent whilst Abbi gathered herself. "Ahem, right, ok, I'm ok, it's just… GOD I'm SO annoyed that I'm upset. I'm angry more than anything"

"Just give yourself a minute; it's ok to be emotional. Whenever you're ready."

After a few moments, Abbi leaned forward and rested her elbows on her knees; she was playing with the tissue I had given her. "Look. Everyone knows I wanna be a boy, right? So why the hell is everyone giving me a hard time over it?"

"Ok, so you feel that everyone is giving you a hard time about wanting to be a boy. Do they say why they don't agree?"

"Pat (Abbi's Foster mother) just says I'm being stupid, the social worker doesn't say anything and CAMHS just keep saying I'm too young to know but I've already started to get boobs and have periods and the longer I wait, the more difficult it will be. And Pat won't let me wear a tuxedo to my Prom and she won't let me have *this* cut" Abbi grabbed her hair in a fist and yanked it hatefully. "And I've got so much to do, it's just too much to do in the time I've got, and my friends are always on at me saying that I boss them about, I don't. And my sister is self-harming, so I have to sort that out as well. Then there's Uni. What if I decide that I don't want to go to Uni? What will I do then? I want to travel but if I don't go to Uni and get a decent job, I won't be able to afford to travel, but then I might get too settled in my job and miss the opportunity of going travelling. And I've got GCSE's coming up, how will I find the time to revise? Oh, and then there's the young explorers camp which is, guess when? Straight after my exams so I need to think about that while I'm doing my exams, in fact, I might just cancel it. And then the worst thing is the bus! The school bus is just SO annoying, people just look at me and stare at me and I hate it. I get so angry I want to hit them all and throw them off the bus so I can be on my own, and, yeh, so, well, yeh, that's it basically" Abbi sat back in her chair laughing. "See what a mess my life is?"

"Wow, I feel exhausted listening to that Abbi, I can only imagine how exhausting it must be to carry all of that worry around with you. How do feel now that you've said it all out loud?"

"I actually feel better because no one has just sat and let me say it before. It's kinda cool" Abbi smiled to herself.

We spent the remainder of the session trying to break down some of Abbi's worries and anxieties and to look at which ones she could file away for another day and which ones she felt needed to be on the urgent pile. Of all her worries, Abbi decided that her journey to school on the bus was the most urgent. We looked at some mindfulness techniques for Abbi to try. I suggested she download some apps onto her phone and listen to them on the bus. Abbi was grateful and as she left, she said she felt a lot better. I, on the other hand, felt useless bewildered and muddled.

I knew little more about Abbi than what Jean had told me that day and, had I not known about the transgender issues and being gay, I would have said that Abbi's greatest concern was an anxiety reaction triggered from many sources. This coupled with the knowledge I *did* have, along with the intervention of social services and foster parents sparked my interest. Could it be that Abbi had suffered some early trauma which she was now responding to with her anxiety? I felt that Abbi's foster mother and CAMHS had fixated on the transgender issue, who wouldn't? But what if Abbi's response was that of a "mother" trying to get control of her "family" only in this case the "family" was friends, school, exams, etc? What if Abbi wanting to be male came from her belief that men had control or held things together? I wondered if the early separation from Abbi's mother and possibly father would be the link I was looking for. What was to come, I learned, was all this and more.

2

Abbi and I spent the next few sessions working on her anxiety response on the school bus and in other scenarios, along with her love of order and control. Abbi learned mindfulness techniques to help focus her mind when she was on the bus and she also listened to short meditations. We learned to use her need for order to Abbi's advantage and she made sticker posters at home and lever arch folders which were beautifully separated into subjects to help with her revision. Abbi had always shied away from her obsession with order, thinking it was something to be quashed but once she learned how to use it mindfully, she would happily clean the house or the cars when she felt stressed to help her get some clarity. When Abbi would become anxious, she would look at her sticker poster and her lever arch files and remind herself that all was well. Abbi was also practising mindfulness and meditation daily and finding that it helped to slow her thinking down.

There were many bumps in the road for Abbi, but she became better at talking them through and staying with the subject matter in hand and not raising 10 other issues. Everything was going well.

One day, not long before Abbi's GCSE's were due to begin, she came to see me and we were talking about her prom and the fact that her foster mother, Pat had agreed that she could wear a tuxedo if that was what she really wanted. As we had spent some time working on Abbi's rather brusque approach and how she might tone it down particularly when talking to Pat as they seemed to clash a little, I was keen to hear how this had developed. "That's great news Abbi! You must be so pleased?" As I looked at Abbi, I noticed two things. Firstly, I noticed she was biting her lip and raising her eyebrows in a mock defensive manner, as if she was about to deliver bad news. Secondly...was that? Yes, it was. Very discreet but it was indeed makeup! "What now?" I said in defeat.

Abbi began to laugh. "Well, erm, you see. Well, I think I want to wear a dress and, yeh, that's it"

"Ok, do you have a picture then?" Abbi excitedly pulled out her phone and started swiping and tapping.

"They're not the best pictures but here goes." Abbi showed me several pictures of a stunning young woman in a pale green satin floor length dress akin to the 1920's style of Ginger Rogers. The dress clung exactly where it needed to cling. It showed the girl's figure beautifully but without being too revealing. The front of the dress was a high cowl neck which was cut across her collar bone before falling in icy green waterfalls which synched in at the waist giving way to sheer satin which tightly covered her flat stomach before falling to the floor. The back was also a waterfall effect but revealing the top half of her back. The back fell seamlessly to the top of her bottom where the dress clung modestly before falling away to a train at the back which settled like a beautiful glistening pool around her feet. Her hair was lazily tied in a top knot, but her look would overshadow any red-carpet siren. This was Abbi, in all her glory, her body on show in womanly form and I was fascinated to know how she had felt when she looked at herself.

"Abbi, you look beautiful, you really do, how do you feel in it?"

"Well, it was really weird, you see, Pat took me to the suit hire shop to look at tuxedos and they do dresses too. Pat made a deal with me that I could try on a suit but just to please her, she asked could I try on a dress too. And, well, there you have it. I really liked it and it felt comfortable too. Mind you, I do have one thing to add which will make it "me"" Abbi swiped her phone and showed me a final picture of her jauntily holding up the hem of her dress to reveal a great big pair of black Doctor Martens boots.

"Yes Abbi, that really *is* "you" it's just great" This was exactly the right moment for me to broach the subject of the transgender issue which had barely been mentioned during our 8 or so sessions together so far.

"So, Abbi. It feels like a good time to ask you about your feelings around the transgender process. Do you mind if we explore this?" Abbi became a little fidgety in her chair and her skin began to redden.

"Yeh, we really need to talk about it don't we. It's just that, well men seem to get what they want in life whereas women, basically.... don't"

"So, you feel that if you were to be a man, you would get what you want? Have more options?" Abbi had tears in her eyes, and she looked up to the ceiling trying to control them. I reached for the tissues and offered her one. As she took it, she sighed as if she were annoyed with herself.

"Men have everything." Abbi started to sob.

"Have you witnessed this before Abbi? Where a man or men have everything?" Still sobbing, Abbi nodded slowly." Can you tell me about it?" Abbi was now extremely distressed, and it took her a few moments to compose herself.

"My...Uncle...and... Dad. With Sammi. They...they...did things to her!" As she completed the statement, Abbi's words were almost undecipherable, but she went on. "The medicine. She was ill...they said...we stayed in the lounge. She screamed...I had a chest infection when I was older...I was terrified! She...she didn't...he...and mom...mom did nothing...and now...she is so fucked up that she has to live in a special home!" Abbi's tears were becoming replaced by venomous anger. "She just sat there, and fucking did NOTHING! Who does that?" I was trying to stay with Abbi and understand what she was telling me. As the horror of the story unfolded, I had to be careful that asking for clarification wasn't merely to serve my own curiosity, but I also had to understand the story and who Sammi was as well as exactly what had gone on. Abbi calmed down after a few minutes. "I want you to know the story" she gasped with a last push of energy.

"Ok, I've got an idea and I think you might like this too. How about we study a timeline of your life from your earliest memory until now? Everything that you can remember good or bad, I'll make notes while you speak and then we can see what we get?" I often use this process with young people as they tend to forget information which may be important, they also get lost in the story rather than how they felt at the time which is where the timeline can be used to great effect to take them back to a time or place.

Abbi was the middle child with an older sister, Sammi and a younger sister Lexi. Abbi's early life had been happy. She shared fond memories of walking to and from school with mom, Sammi and Lexi and stopping off at the local sweet shop to choose a sweet to eat on the way home. The home was a happy one and Abbi was a keen artist, often making paintings and drawings for her parents which Mom would stick around the house. Apart from a few other non-incidental childhood memories all had been quiet and happy for the first few years of Abbi's life. Abbi's uncle had come to live with them after someone had set fire to his home with him in it. Abbi never questioned this. Abbi couldn't seem to remember a change in the way things were, except that she had become aware that her older sister Sammi had to be taken off sometimes to have medicine administered for an infection. Sammi would cry when mom told her it was time and Abbi would listen as she screamed when her Dad and Uncle went into her room to give the medication. This went on for some time and Sammi had to be left alone afterwards to let the medicine work even though Abbi always wanted to go in and see her to give her a hug. Abbi would draw pictures for Sammi of sparkling eyes, tear free and give them to her in the hope that Sammi would feel better soon and not have to cry any more. Sammi always cried at the pictures.

One day, several cars came, and police and social workers entered the home. Abbi remembered people everywhere and three policemen picked her, Sammi and Lexi up in each of their arms and marched out to three waiting cars. Lexi at 6, was too young to realise what was happening and Abbi didn't know about Sammi, but Abbi remembered being terrified that these people were taking her away. She grabbed her mother's clothing as her mother chased the policeman carrying her. Abbi was screaming and she held onto her mother's jumper as if her life depended on it. The policeman was obviously trying not to hurt Abbi but maintained a strong grip on her. As Abbi was lowered into the car, her mother was pulled in too and she lay on her back across the back seat trying to grab Abbi from the policeman. The social worker who was waiting inside the car tried to calm Abbi's mother but to no avail. It was only when another policeman arrived that Abbi's mother was removed from the car. She was made to put her hands behind her back and the policeman placed handcuffs on her and marched her off to a waiting police car. The next thing Abbi saw were her father and uncle also being marched off by police with their hands behind their backs and then lots of people going into their house wearing white overalls. Abbi's car started to move, and she began to scream again kicking and punching the social worker in the back of the car. "Abbi, please stop, you're hurting me, stop it!"

The social worker managed to grab Abbi's legs and hold them down with the rest of her being restrained by the seatbelt. Once Abbi had realised physical resistance was futile, she broke down and sobbed. All three girls were taken to emergency foster care and that is where Abbi remained until she went to live with Pat. There were meetings and meetings and then more meetings. Abbi found out that her sister Sammi, who was 10 had been consistently and violently sexually abused by her Uncle and Father and others from the age of 3. The abuse was filmed and sold by Abbi's parents. Sammi had become increasingly withdrawn and ill and concerns were raised by the school nurse which was reported to the police. Sammi has been left with significant physical and emotional injuries which have resulted in her having to live in sheltered accommodation with carers. Abbi does not know the full extent or detail of the case and will be able to request the case notes once she is 18. On the day they were taken into care, Abbi was 8.

Abbi admitted that she wasn't sure how much of the story was a memory and how much had been fabricated in her mind. The lack of information had led Abbi to believe the worst scenarios to fill in the gaps and, from what she had told me, I feared that Abbi's version was very close to the truth. Abbi was, at this time extremely angry towards her parents and spent many sessions trying to make sense of what they had done. We used some basic anger management techniques to help Abbi to recognise her anger first of all so that she could understand what she was angry about and why. As Abbi had responded well to mindfulness and meditation techniques, I used visualisation for her anger. I asked Abbi to try and describe her anger to me, to tell me what it might look like if she had to draw it. "A giant penis" Abbi's face screwed up in tears as she said the words. "Oh god...I'm so disgusting. How could I think that? Penises are so gross, and I think about them all the time!" Abbi was distraught and embarrassed. I, on the other hand saw this as a massive breakthrough and something we could really begin to work with.

"Abbi, you are doing brilliantly well. I need you to stay with your vision. You say that this is your anger. Tell me more about the penis" I already had an idea of what Abbi was going to say but I had to get her to say it so that we had utter transparency. Through sobs Abbi spat the words out as if she were mustering the final 1% of her energy capacity.

"Raping me" If it were possible, Abbi sobbed even more. I passed her another tissue and sat silently in front of her while she sobbed 8 years of silence and disgust into it.

Abbi talked about how a man's penis was all powerful and could do what it wanted, and no one could stop it. She felt an anger towards it but also helpless to it. Abbi tried really hard with her visualisations to imagine the penis being put away into pants or becoming smaller so it could barely be seen. Abbi had been ruled by this vision for so long that it had even infected her own view of her gender and her self-image.

Abbi slowly came to realise that she did not want to become a man and even began to talk about boys that she liked. For a while, Abbi was calm. She sailed through her GCSE's and we took a break from our sessions whilst she enjoyed study leave. One sunny afternoon when I was at Abbi's school, I heard the door to the student support centre open and a breathy voice I recognised "Is Sarah here today?"

The next thing I heard were thunderous footsteps clambering up the stairs towards my room. My door was ajar, signifying I'm free and in burst a ball of energy, out of breath, rosy cheeked and elated. "I've finished!" Abbi punched the air with her fists and danced on the spot. "I did it! I did it!" I laughed and rejoiced with Abbi but before I got the chance to speak, she was gone. Tapping down the stairs two or three at a time and out the door. I got up and looked out of the window just in time to see Abbi running over to a group of similarly excited girls who greeted her with screams and hugs. This small gesture from Abbi meant the World to me. Not just for egotistical reasons. Of course, to see a person experience an intense journey and to share that satisfies a part of me which allows me to congratulate myself on a job well done. Mostly though, I felt happy for her. She had, for the first time in her life, been able to verbalise her pain. Exploring feelings of anger, disgust, fear, love and how they had all become distorted by external factors beyond her control.

3

Abbi had secured her GCSE marks and had started the sixth form. A keen debater and philosopher, she had chosen Religious Education, Sociology and Drama for her A Levels. We had agreed that when Abbi returned to sixth form, should she need to see me, she could self-refer via the school's pastoral support service. A few weeks into the new school year, I had a referral from Abbi. She had stated that she was struggling with her "A" Levels and wasn't sure if this was the correct route for her to take, she wanted to talk things through with

someone.

When Abbi appeared, she looked very different to the last time I had seen her just a couple of months earlier. No longer confined by the school uniform, it was interesting to see Abbi expressing herself through clothes. She wore black jeans which clung to her long slim legs and a grey loose-fitting top covered with a dark navy waterproof jacket. On her feet were black Converse trainers. Her image seemed to reflect her almost carefree attitude to external looks and I had an image of her dressing that morning and grabbing the closest items of clothing to hand with barely a glance in the mirror. There were a couple of distinct differences, however, which seemed to contradict my appraisal of Abbi's clothing. These being her hair which now brushed across the tops of her shoulders in a straight bob and her face which was now bore a very natural brush of colour on her cheeks, a flick of mascara and the all-important pencilled eyebrows. As Abbi sat before me, her visual image at least was saying to me that she was far more at ease with herself and that she had invested in her look in a way which suited her personality.

Inside the Teenage Mind

"So, Abbi...first of all congratulations on your GCSE's. Tell me how things are going" Abbi sat in silence and stared at the wall. Her eyes filled with tears and her neck became blotchy.

"Rubbish. I can't do it. And Pat says if I don't go to Uni, I'll have to leave and go into care!"

Abbi had a habit of misinterpreting some information and subsequently dramatizing the facts to fill in the gaps. A habit she had developed to fill in the gaps of her own life so far. We had to pick apart what was really going on here.

I looked at Abbi as if to question her comment and she broke into a laugh. "It's true!" she insisted.

"Ok, let's break this down a little. So, you say that sixth form is rubbish and you can't do it? And that if you don't go to Uni Pat says you'll have to leave and go into care, correct?" Abbi nodded.

"Let's start with sixth form, what is it that is rubbish?"

"I don't know, it's just everything. I'm not enjoying Sociology and RE is hard. Drama is ok I guess but I feel

trapped and that I can't do it"

"So, you say you feel trapped? Tell me more about that"

"Yeh, it's just too hard and I've got no friends and I don't even know what I want to do or if I want to go to Uni at all. Well, I sort of do want to go to Uni but...well...you know...there's this guy...and he's going off to Australia to Uni so he'll be leaving me just like everyone else does" I shook my head from side to side in disbelief. I was trying desperately to keep up with Abbi whilst at the same time trying to decipher what was really going on for her.

"Whoa, wait a minute, let me catch up Abbi. You've got no friends and... Who's the guy?" Abbi broke into laughter as I repeated her words back to her with an obvious tone of my own absolute loss for words.

As Abbi's face changed at the mention of "the guy" it became clear to me that this may well be the cause of her angst. "He's called Rich and... well yeh, he's, well, he's really nice" As Abbi spoke, her cheeks flushed with colour and she could do nothing to stop the perma-smile on her face. "But he's going off to Australia to study something to do with Marine life or something and then he'll be gone."

We talked about Abbi's feelings for Rich and how they had been a complete shock to her. She had never before found a male attractive and wasn't sure that she even did find him attractive as the feelings were so new to her. Rich knew nothing of Abbi's past but had been extremely patient with her regarding the physical side of things. Everything seemed perfect for Abbi but all she could focus on was the inevitable end of the relationship when it had barely yet begun. Abbi confessed that thinking about Rich jetting off to Australia had ignited her own desire to travel and when she had mentioned to Pat, her foster mother about the possibility of a gap year, Pat had expressed concern about the funding situation for Abbi and how this would affect her care allowances and benefits. Pat had explained that once Abbi was eighteen, she could either stay with Pat and in full time education or she could leave and move into her own place having control of her own care allowance. Abbi soon came to realise that her situation hadn't been as bad as she first thought but that she was indeed panicked about how her relationship with Rich would develop physically. We were coming to the end of the session, so we agreed to pick this up at our next session. Abbi had expressed fear at seeing Rich's penis and the thought of touching it scared her too. I asked Abbi to focus not on Rich's body but on her own. I sensed that Abbi had never really gotten to know herself as a woman and her physical self-awareness seemed very low. I asked Abbi to take a good look at her body in the mirror and also to explore it with her hands. What feels nice, what tickles etc. I reminded Abbi that before she experiences someone else's body, she should know her own.

Abbi went on to have several intimate experiences with Rich, some of which she enjoyed. I was very careful not to draw any similarities between this sort of sexual encounter and that of her sister at the hands of her father and uncle but at the same time I wanted her to understand that there was a distinct difference between the two. We gently discussed these encounters as and when they arose, but events overtook us as Rich ended their relationship, causing untold hurt and upset for Abbi.

Once again, we worked through her attitude to loss and endings and her need for control. After many weeks and months, Abbi finally came to see her affair with Rich for what it was, an extremely important chapter in her life which taught her many things. Abbi and Rich even became friends.

Although I knew that Abbi would undoubtedly need therapy on and off for many years to come, by and large, there seemed to be longer periods of time in between her meltdowns and they also lessened in their extremity.

One of Abbi's major blows came from her younger sister Lexi who, although she had been more shielded from the events surrounding their parents had nonetheless suffered the emotional trauma which showed itself in the shape of self-harm and bulimia. Lexi had announced that she wished to contact their parents, and this had caused an almighty family row. Abbi simply could not understand why her sister could do this and why she should want anything to do with these hideous evil people. Abbi's anger had reared its head once more and she had noticed that she had become venomous and hateful towards others, wanting them to argue with her. "I just feel so angry with everyone all the time" Abbi seemed distressed by her anger and her negativity as she was normally an upbeat bubbly girl. We decided to revisit some anger management techniques.

"Ok Abbi let's have a look at this anger of yours. Tell me what you are feeling if it's still the same vision or whether it has changed" Abbi closed her eyes for a few moments to focus. "

It feels like blackness pressing down on me, like I can't breathe. It's like a black fog"

"Ok that's brilliant, so you see a black fog which presses down on you and makes you struggle to breathe. Let's just stay with it for a moment and acknowledge its presence" Abbi's eyes remained closed as she gently nodded her head. "The idea now Abbi is for us to take control of the fog and try and change it. Can we try and make it lighter, a little less dense first?"

Visualising anger or anxiety in this way and then changing the image is extremely effective and has often given the students I work with the confidence to face their anger or anxiety head on and change it. When used effectively, it can be life changing.

"Yes, it's getting thinner now" I had no doubt that Abbi would work well in this way as she was becoming increasingly adept at mindfulness meditation techniques.

"Ok, can we look at changing the colour? Imagine droplets of pink coming into the black"

"Yes, it's quite pretty actually" Abbi was smiling.

"How is your anger now?"

"I feel better"

"Great. Abbi, I want you to practice this visualisation every time you feel yourself getting angry and even practice it when you aren't feeling so angry, maybe when you go to bed you might want to spend a few minutes doing it then"

This technique is one to use in the moment and can help with outbursts of anger. The cause of the anger, however, still needs looking into and I always approach anger management by first teaching techniques to enable people to feel more in control and then delving into the reasons for the anger. With Abbi it was easy to see why she would be angry and why she blamed her parents for everything bad in her life but as our sessions went on, it was clear that anger was only one of the emotions Abbi had and it stood alongside guilt, fear, shame and disgust.

When Abbi had first began to express her anger in outbursts as a child of 9, she had been referred for counselling. Her young age and her lack of self-awareness had meant that she had not really benefitted from the sessions. Another blow for Abbi was that she had been told constantly by social workers and by her foster parents that, as she had not actually suffered abuse herself, why should she be upset. I had shuddered when Abbi told me this, feeling angry that others may judge what constitutes trauma in a situation like this. I had to put my feelings aside and help Abbi make sense of her own experience.

Abbi told me that when she was younger, she would pretend, in her mind, that she had also been abused as this would help to alleviate some of the guilt, she felt that her sister had been the only one attacked. Abbi also bravely admitted that she sometimes wished that *she* had been picked for the "attention" that was afforded to her sister. It was perhaps our most difficult and draining session.

"I'm disgusting! I wanted it to happen to me! And when I get angry, I feel like I want to have sex. Oh my god what's wrong with me?"

"There's nothing wrong at all Abbi, go on, you're safe here"

"So, sometimes I pick an argument with people when I know they will retaliate. But no one ever says what I need them to say" Abbi was sobbing by now, her head in her hands which rested on her legs. Her shoulders were shuddering, and she was crying in an almost primeval manner. Jean appeared at the door and gestured to me to check if all was ok. I gave Jean the thumbs up, she returned the gesture and went away.

"I want them to tell me I'm worthless and useless… and shit…and not worth being alive, like a piece of shit on the pavement…and… then…" Abbi was almost screaming at this point, her sobs were coming from a place that had been locked away for many years. She was unable to speak any more, she was only able to make helpless sighs and sharp intakes of breath. She was desperately trying to get her words out and it was as if she had to conjure up every ounce of strength to do so.

"And then...I want them to rape me!" the manic sobbing returned, and Abbi sat helpless on her chair, clutching at her forehead, occasionally hitting it in frustration and raw emotion.

"Well done Abbi" was all I could think of to say. My comment was sorely lacking in its impact, but I needed her to know that what had just happened was a good thing. "You've done amazingly well today Abbi, you really have" I gave Abbi a couple of minutes to stop crying and compose herself. She looked exhausted but also lighter.

"I'm just afraid that because I feel like this about, you know, sex, that I'll end up like them"

"Abbi it's perfectly normal that you have a somewhat distorted view of sex and which emotions to attach to it. Your only reference point is anger and negativity. The very fact that you feel the way you do means that you want to look at things differently. What we need to do now is look at these emotions and thoughts and then we can start to make sense of them and see them for what they are, the traumatic memories of a small child locked up in a young adult's body. Until now that is", I smiled at Abbi and she smiled back. My instinct was to take her in my arms and console her, but I knew that this was not the right thing to do; although sometimes working with teenagers the lines are a little blurred. But in this case, it would have been the wrong thing for Abbi who did not look at affection in the same way as me.

4

Abbi and I worked hard over the next few sessions to support her to confront her feelings towards her parents and towards herself. We used a variety of techniques including further visualisations, journal writing and physical punching sessions with Abbi's poor pillow. It was now time, however for Abbi to have a conversation with the part of herself that she had kept locked away in the depths of her mind. It was time for Abbi to meet with her disgust, hatred and fear.

I decided to use something called the empty chair technique which I had learned about many years ago but had not used for some time. It felt like the right thing to do here to help Abbi get some perspective and some control over her feelings. The empty chair technique is where an empty chair is placed opposite the client and the client imagines a particular person is sitting in the chair. The person is not able to respond and must sit and listen until the client tells me that they are finished. I explained the process to Abbi who seemed excited and filled with trepidation in equal measure. We had decided mutually that the first person in the hot seat would be Abbi's father. Abbi turned to face the chair and fidgeted in her own seat nervously. "I feel a bit silly" She turned to me for reassurance.

"Ok Abbi, your Dad is sitting right there, he cannot speak but he can hear you. What is the first thing you would like to ask him?" Abbi adjusted herself and straightened her back, she took a deep breath and tentatively started.

"Why? Hmmmm? Just, Why? Why the hell did you do what you did to Sammi? She was defenceless and you hurt her. Why?"

"Tell your Dad how you feel about him and what happened"

It was at this point that Abbi seemed to change gear. She started to shout and scream at the chair; her hands were gesturing, and she was making fists and pointing accusingly at the chair. She swore profusely and called the chair every derogatory name she could muster. Abbi was spitting as she spoke, and her face became distorted with venom. Her face was crimson red and the veins in her neck popped as she grimaced her way through the 15-minute ordeal. It was truly a form of self-exorcism for her. The hatred that had built up and not been able to show itself was now in full force. No wonder Abbi had not wanted to unleash this part of her before. This was an amazingly fearful site. Abbi stood up and walked around the empty chair pointing and screaming at it. "You're disgusting *DISGUSTING*, do you hear me? You don't deserve to be on this earth, you don't deserve children, and you don't deserve a life because you've taken ours! I hate you I hate you! If you were on fire, I wouldn't even piss on you, you disgusting piece of shit! No, actually shit has a purpose in life to process our waste so you're not even a piece of fucking shit!" I carefully masked a grin which had developed in admiration of Abbi's ability to apply logic to the name calling.

As Abbi came towards the end of her torrent, she sat back on her chair, exhausted and a great big smile came across her face. Abbi was physically out of breath, her tied back hair had escaped in places and had stuck to her clammy forehead. "That was ACE!" said Abbi as she threw her head back and laughed at the ceiling.

Before I could ask if there was anything else Abbi wanted to say, she sat bolt upright and looked once more at the empty chair. "Oh yeah, and another thing, I've finished talking to you now, so FUCK OFF!" Abbi sat back in her chair and folded her arms in front of her body, staring defiantly at the wall to her right. I quietly got up and moved the empty chair back to its original position and opened and closed the door to signify Abbi's father had left. As I did, Abbi said "Yeah, that's it, fuck off back where you came from you evil cunt"

As Abbi turned to face me, she looked elated, defiant, strong. I could see that the process had worked really well for her. "How do you feel Abbi?"

"Amazing, I can't believe how much I enjoyed that. I'm knackered though but in a good way. I feel like I've just done a big poo or had my stomach pumped and all the negative crap came out, it's hard to describe.

As Abbi and I continued our work together, we used the empty chair technique for her mother, her uncle and for the younger version of herself. Abbi told herself or "young Abbi" that what had happened was not her fault and that she had been brave and strong to get where she is today. She also told "young Abbi" that it was ok to remember good times with Mom and Dad because they had happened and every experience that she had, good or bad, had contributed to making her who she was today. Abbi had thanked the young version of herself for just being her.

There were good times and bad for Abbi and, as I recalled earlier, I feel that she will return to therapy at points in her life. At least I can rest assured that Abbi found her encounter with therapy to be positive and helpful and hopefully this will encourage her to seek help should she need it in years to come.

Abbi went on to complete her "A" Levels and secured a place at University studying journalism. A year or so later, Jean had given me a printed article which had been passed on the Head Teacher for the school's achievement collection. The article was a beautiful piece about women and their place in society and in business and had been published in a National Business magazine. It was written by Abbi.

LUCY

Lucy and I had crossed paths before when I was working with one of her friends. There had been an almighty falling out which had affected not only most of the year group but also rippled through the school. The girls involved were the mouthpieces of the school. Loud, brash and intimidating they moved in packs and instilled terror into the rest of the school. The truth of the matter was that they were trying to find their way in the World. In many cases they had been exposed to violence and abuse as well as poverty and irrational parenting. They lacked the tools necessary to make their way through life free from aggression and conflict. As these were their blueprint for survival, their primeval need to protect each other would occasionally erupt into a bloodbath of words and violence towards each other. There was no head of the pride to correct these lionesses; their regard for authority of any kind had long since dwindled. They would laugh in the face of detentions, exclusions and other desperate measures to control their behaviour in a suburban school setting. Their lives outside of school were sometimes dangerous and often without boundaries, having been taught long ago how to fool and lie to anyone outside of the circle, the pride.

Lucy's friend, Chloe had been working with me for a while and had been extremely upset by the falling out. We had decided to see if Lucy would talk to Chloe and sort things out with her. I went to Lucy's class and asked her teacher if I would speak with her. As he called her name, he looked over at her, my eyes followed his as I had not seen Lucy before so wanted to make eye contact with her myself. There Lucy sat, defiant and full of anger. She was hunched in her chair with her arms folded in front of her. With a sigh, Lucy slowly gathered her things and made her way to the door. "Hi Lucy, I'm..."

"Sarah, yeh I know who you are. Am I in trouble?" Lucy almost expected trouble as this was the only form of attention, she got these days.

"No, far from it. I was wondering if you could help me with something." Lucy stopped in her tracks and scowled at me. I was taken aback by her immensely long eye lashes and her crudely made up face. I sensed that she had found the ultimate mask to hide behind in the form of makeup. Lucy's hair was also a main of protection. All one length, Lucy's hair fell to her waist and was thick and blonde with no artificial colouring to spoil its youthful sheen. Lucy reminded me of a warrior princess. She was stocky in build and had strong cat like features. Her cheekbones didn't benefit from or need the thick brown lines drawn under them to contour her face. Her foundation was the wrong colour and gave her pale skin a false orangey brown pallor. Any colour in her lips had been obliterated by thick white concealer but underneath all of this there was a smouldering beauty and resilience. It could not be contained, and it found its conduit in her piercing blue eyes which refused to be dulled or hidden no matter how she tried.

"Help? You? Why?" Lucy, like many of her friends was unfamiliar with the concept of giving anything freely so as not to be exposed in any way. This would make her vulnerable and vulnerability was to be avoided at all costs.

"Well, not me as such, its Chloe..." I paused expecting opposition, but Lucy remained silent. She raised her eyebrows to question me and jauntily flicked her head to one side the way teenagers do. Eventually she sighed and resumed walking. I took this as a signal that, so far at least, she was willing to listen. "Chloe seems really upset about what happened between you. She says that she thinks you hate her and never want to be friends again."

"Well that's just stupid. I'm annoyed with her; she's behaved like a dick, but I don't hate her." It seemed that all these lionesses needed were a little time to cool down. I never did get to the bottom of the argument but when Lucy entered the room and looked at Chloe, they said sorry simultaneously and then laughed. I left the girls alone to chat for a few minutes and they emerged laughing and sharing a drink. Their demeanour had changed from aggressive and looking for trouble to relaxed and giggly. Peace had been restored.

It would be the next school year before Lucy and I would meet again. There had been incidents where Lucy's anger had gotten out of control and she had hit a boy in class. She was also generally rude and aggressive and thundering towards a permanent exclusion. The school pupil support team had tried everything including trying to reason with Lucy's equally aggressive mother, but everyone was running out of options. They knew that there must have been a trigger for Lucy's sudden downturn, but she was not willing to say. As is so often the case with school counsellors, I was the last resort and Lucy's last chance. I was asked to do some anger management work with Lucy and we had just two weeks to sort this out, if Lucy was aggressive once more in this time period she would be out of the school and if there had been no improvement at the end of two weeks she would be gone.

I see many persistently mal-behaved children who are often the product of weak parenting and a society which sometimes puts over hashed human rights above basic rules for existing in a social and global community. To hear a 15-year-old boy, accuse a teacher of threatening him when the teacher asks him to leave the classroom otherwise, he will have to call for assistance; after he has constantly disrupted the learning of the whole class is but one example. Too many times I hear statements like "It's not my fault, how am I supposed to behave when I hate school!" Time after time, these young people are flanked by their equally self-righteous parents who complain at being asked to come along and talk to teachers about their child's behaviour, telling the teachers..." You're the school, you're getting paid, you sort it out!" This, along with increasing cuts to resources and never-ending red tape is increasingly making teaching a career to be avoided.

Lucy, however, was different. Feisty? Yes. Likeable? Yes. A candidate for permanent exclusion? No. Despite her rawness and abrasive way, Lucy was, overall respectful and functioned mostly within the rules of the school.

Lucy entered my room and fiddled around with her large bag for a few moments. Eventually, she put the bag to one side and in her hands, was a packet of mints. Lucy undid the wrapper and offered the mints to me. "No thanks"

"Do you mind if I have one?" Eating and drinking outside of break and lunchtime was prohibited but I often let students eat and drink with me especially if it helps them to relax.

"No, you carry on. So, Lucy, what brings you here and how do you think I can help?" I had decided to start working straight away as time was of the essence here.

"You can't help. No one can. I'm a nutter and no one can help me."

"You say you're a nutter, that's a strong word. Tell me why you think this?"

"I don't think it, I know it! I'm being haunted and I can't tell anyone"

"Haunted? Tell me about that"

"My stepdad, Mike, he died, well we were told he died but I know he's still out there, I see him. I saw him this morning by the lake"

"It's quite normal to see, hear or feel the presence of a loved one after they have passed. Tell me more about Mike."

Lucy went on to tell me that Mike had died around 5 weeks ago. He had recently been released from prison and had committed suicide. She and her mother had not known that Mike had died because they no longer had contact with him. He was in prison for brutally beating Lucy's mother whom he almost killed and whilst he was in prison, they had moved away from the neighbourhood in which Lucy grew up, to start a new life. Lucy's mother had found out via social media that Mike was dead almost two weeks after the event. Understandably perhaps, Lucy's mother was pleased to be released from Mike and had celebrated the news. Lucy had no choice but to visibly react in the same way. Inside Lucy's mind, however, things were different. She felt confused at not being able express her true feelings, her mother would go mad if she knew how Lucy felt and what she was thinking. I reassured Lucy that anything she told me would be in confidence and added,

"You know, it's ok to be upset that Mike is dead. Even though what he did was terrible, he was still your Stepdad and he did those things to your mom, not you."

"But he did it to me as well" she replied in a quiet voice. As I looked across at Lucy, she had shrunken in size and to all intents and purposes she had regressed from a 14-year-old to a 10-year-old. The Lucy that sat before me was overlaid with a vision in my mind of a small terrified girl clutching a battered teddy bear, tears layered upon dried tears which had stung her cheeks and made them crimson. So small and still trying to make herself even smaller, better still, invisible.

I rallied myself and returned to the present moment with Lucy. I noticed her deep in thought so left a silence for her to process this new experience.

After a while, I ventured "How do you feel Lucy?" Her eyes turned to mine and I sensed she was stuck somewhere in between the small frightened girl and the toughened warrior princess that she had had to become. Which would she choose?

"I'm alright, I'm not gonna cry if that's what ya think. Don't do crying"

"Ok, you seemed to be in thought back there, is there anything you want to talk about?"

"Is it wrong that I loved him?"

"Do *you* think you're wrong to love him?"

"I dunno, I mean he was pretty vile, but he wasn't a shit dad like my birth dad. He loved us, in his own way and, for a while things were pretty good. When he got with my mom, she had me and my two brothers. I was 5 and they were 8 and 10. He took us all on and never complained, he called me his princess, and I was his favourite. My mom said I could always wrap him around my little finger" Lucy held up her little finger and looked at it wistfully. "Anyway, I suppose I didn't realise at first but him and mom used to have really bad arguments and sometimes they would throw things around. My brothers always took me upstairs and distracted me and I didn't take much notice. Mom would always be crying after they argued and sometimes Mike would go out and we would help her clean up the mess. When I got a little bit older, I tried to stay downstairs when they argued. I don't know why; I think something inside me knew that mom was in danger, but I didn't know what. It worked for a bit and Mike would back off when I asked him to stop. And so, it worked...until it didn't work" Lucy shuffled uncomfortably in her chair.

We were coming to the end of the session and I wanted to make sure that Lucy didn't go somewhere emotionally that would cause her problems and jeopardise her time at school. I decided to stop her at this point. "Lucy you've done amazingly well today. You've managed to talk about something that is obviously really hard for you and I hope it's helped a bit. Would you like to come and see me again to talk more?" Lucy nodded her head and rose from her chair gathering her bag and coat. There was no emotion from her as she left but as she was closing the door behind her, she said "Thank you Sarah"

2

Thankfully, Lucy made the two weeks without further incident and we were able to continue our work together.

During that time, and as our work continued, Lucy told me in more detail about the abuse and terror that she and her family had suffered at the hands of this man who had not only physically abused all of them but once Lucy's mother had the courage to leave him, had stalked them and continued his reign of terror in other ways.

Lucy told me how he would stand outside their house and stare in the windows. As his confidence grew, the encounters became more fearful. Lucy had told me of how he used a screwdriver to unfasten the handle of the back door one night, taking the lock to pieces and boldly walking into the house, entering every bedroom to say "hello" whilst laughing and taunting them. "You'll never be rid of me. You're my family and you always will be"

Lucy's mother contacted the police and they had agreed to make regular checks on the house as well as installing other anti-intruder gadgets such as an alarm and a safe room. Lucy reported having been beyond terrified when one evening a policeman came to check on them. As Lucy's mother opened the door, Mike stood before her in a police uniform, grinning. No matter how they tried, the family could not be free from Mike. He would turn up at the school gates, standing in the back garden or in the supermarket.

Eventually, Mike was apprehended by the police and went to prison for a short term. Lucy was not sure of the charges.

"Don't you see Lucy?" I told her, "It makes sense that you feel Mike is haunting you because in your mind nothing can keep him away, not even death"

"So, do you think he's real then?"

"I think you keep him real and you keep him alive. That's great news for us though because it also means that you have the power to be rid of him once and for all. This time, it's you who gets rid of him"

3

Lucy and I worked over the following weeks and months using a range of techniques which blended bereavement counselling with anger and anxiety management. Lucy was able to grieve for Mike and say goodbye to him in a loving way and this helped her to also dismiss the evil presence of Mike that she felt was haunting her. Lucy began to soften around the edges, and we developed a very close relationship.

I had talked to my clinical supervisor about Lucy and my affection for her and she had reminded me that it was Lucy's strength and resilience that I was drawn to and for this reason she did not need my pity or any help beyond that which I gave in the consulting room.

Despite the warnings, my affection for Lucy grew and I made the fateful mistake of integrating my own agenda into our work together.

I knew that Lucy would more than likely fail her GCSE's and that because of her family life, her options would be very limited. I wanted to help Lucy; I wanted to give her a helping hand.

Anyone who knows me knows that I can be extremely persuasive, and I usually get what I want from family friends and colleagues. I never take this for granted and never use it detrimentally, on the contrary I usually rope everyone into my current saviour project, be it abused animals, saving bees or, in this case helping a bright young girl to achieve her full potential.

Sarah Terry

I have many friends who have their own businesses or are successful in their chosen careers and so I decided to enlist some help. I used Facebook to contact all my friends and told them about Lucy's plight. I painted the picture I saw which was an intelligent, resilient feisty young woman who through no fault of her own was destined for a life of poverty. She had no contacts or support at home; she needed help that only we could offer her. The replies came thick and fast with offers of money, hair styling, clothes, contacts for work and even an offer of a college interview. I chose not to discuss this with my clinical supervisor for fear she would not understand although in reality I worried that she would talk me out of it.

By now it was too late, I was embroiled in my fantasy that thanks to me Lucy would have the life I wanted for her. I spent time looking through the responses, setting up times that Lucy could attend various appointments for work experience and liaising with Lucy as to when she would be free. Her first appointment was with my close friend and hairdresser Ruby who had agreed not only for Lucy to come and work with her for the day but also that she would treat Lucy to a hair do at the end of the day. By now, Lucy had completed her GCSE's and was at home. I collected her to take her to Ruby's. As I sat outside Lucy's house I looked around at the unkempt gardens and the boarded windows and I felt uncomfortable. I saw net curtains twitching and heard a few dogs barking. Lucy's own front door was covered over with metal sheeting, why I was unsure; and all the curtains were closed. Eventually Lucy emerged looking perturbed and as she made her way towards the car, she kept looking back at the door which was ajar. There was clearly an argument of some kind ensuing. Eventually, Lucy reached the car and the front door slammed shut.

"Hi Lucy, how are you?"

"I'm ok, how are you?" Lucy was sombre and didn't seem at all excited.

If it were possible that I could have been any more blinkered then clearly, I was on this day. Without realising it, I was drawing Lucy into my world, a world which she never asked to be part of and for which she was not at all equipped. I ignored this. It would be latest in a long line of mistakes that I had made at Lucy's expense.

"My mom has asked me to ask you something"

"Ok, what?"

"She wants to know if I'm getting paid for today"

"Oh right, well, no, we hadn't planned that, it was more to get an experience and then don't forget you get your hair done at the end of the day"

"I can't buy fags with a posh hairdo, can I? It's no use to me and mom needs fags"

I noticed a change in Lucy's attitude. Throughout our work together, Lucy had always been extremely protective of her mother and would often give her the pocket money she received from her grandparents to buy food or electricity. This was different however; it was almost like Lucy's mother was speaking through her. The open and amiable Lucy who had worked with me at the school was gone. Although Lucy retained a respectful politeness with me, it was becoming clear that she now saw me as "one of them" rather than an ally.

I felt my stomach sink and my mouth went dry. My logical and trained mind was trying to tell my overly sensitive and over attached mind something but for some reason I wasn't listening to the warning signs.

We arrived at Ruby's and she greeted us with her usual warm openness. Ruby, like me was in her early 40's and had a long and established career in the hair care industry. This shop was her livelihood and she treated her customers like family. "We've got some lovely ladies in today Lucy, so it should be a nice day for you" Lucy stood in the doorway with her coat folded over her arms which were crossed in front of her. She stared at the floor barely making eye contact with Ruby. Ruby looked at me with an eyebrow raised but remained staunch. "Right then, let's get started. How's your tea making? That's important so shall we get the kettle on?" Ignoring Ruby's attempt at humour, Lucy shrugged her shoulders and turned to face me.

"What time are you picking me up?" I felt Ruby's eyes on me, and my cheeks flushed red with embarrassment. I was frozen like a rabbit in torch light whilst my mind was trying to make an excuse for Lucy's behaviour to one of my closest friends.

"Bloody hell, with a face like that you'll be scaring the customers away! Are you sure you want to come here love?" Once again, Lucy turned to me.

"Are you gonna ask her?"

"Ask her what?"

"For cash instead of my hair done?" Time slowed down almost to a stop as I rose above the three of us and looked down on what I saw. Ruby, eyes wide open in shock and about to give Lucy her answer; Lucy staring woefully at the floor as if she were being forced to work in the poor house, and me with my face posed for laughing or crying or both.

I had ignored my own gut and my own training. What I had done could be classed as at the least unethical and at its most serious unacceptable professional conduct. I had ignored my own mother asking me if I was too personally involved, my husband questioning whether this was part of my job and worst of all, my son telling me that he felt like Lucy was my other child and what more that she was my favourite. What a mess but this was my mess and it didn't need to become Ruby's mess too.

Before Ruby could give Lucy her answer which, knowing Ruby would be to the point and not sparing any detail regarding what she thought, I interjected, "Ruby, I'm sorry this is my mistake. Lucy I'm sorry, we need to go, come on I'll take you home. Ruby, I'll call you later" As we hurriedly rushed back to my car, I was thinking of the other apologetic phone calls I would have to make to no fewer than 6 friends and colleagues with whom I had lined up work experience, informal chats and visits to places of work and interviews. The biggest apology I would need to make was to Lucy, poor Lucy who wouldn't even realise what had gone on.

"What was all that about? I mean, don't get me wrong, I didn't want to work with the old bag anyway but still, why did you make me leave?"

"Look Lucy, I'm sorry, really sorry about all of this. I think I've pushed you into something you didn't really want, and it's made you unhappy."

"Why? What do you mean?" I felt like a useless idiot. I couldn't even answer her. What the hell *did* I mean? How could I explain my stupidity to her?

I tried in the best way I could to say that perhaps Lucy should spend a few weeks over the summer thinking about what she wanted and then she should contact the school who would be able to support her if she felt she needed this.

"Ok, well, Mom's getting two kittens this weekend so that'll keep me busy as I'll need to train them. Maybe I'll see you around" With that, Lucy was getting out of my car and walking out of my life without a second thought. She closed the car door behind her and started back towards her house. Just as she reached about halfway between her house and my car, Lucy stopped in her tracks and after a short pause began to walk back towards my car. I let the window down and Lucy poked her head inside the car. "Thanks Sarah, for everything".

My eyes stung with tears as I drove away from Lucy's house. I had made a fool of myself and nearly of Lucy. I tried to tell myself that I had done it with the best of intentions, but this didn't work. I had acted selfishly and had lost sight of Lucy and her needs. I tried to force her into a mould that I had created, and it was suffocating her and putting her into an even more vulnerable position.

I carried the shame of what I had done for months. I questioned my ability to work with young adults and compared myself to hardened teachers who had been worn down over the years until they had become nothing more than box tickers completing task after task like automatons. Perhaps they had a point, perhaps I should become more like them, I should learn to care less.

I decided eventually that this journey should be seen as just that and also a valuable lesson to learn. I could hear my words echoing around my head as they had been said many times before to my clients. "What can you take away from this? How can you improve what you do from now on?"

I learned, or should I say; I re-learned that the reason why counselling works is because of the professional relationship and the non-involvement with the everyday life of the client. I had crossed that boundary and taken Lucy with me. I had done the very thing that I often tell others not to do, I had gone into "rescue" mode. I was trying to *rescue* Lucy from something which she had not asked to be rescued from and quite possibly didn't need rescuing from.

Lucy, as my supervisor had told me, was a strong resilient young lady who did not need my pity. She had utilised her counselling experience to help her process a difficult time in her life and was more than capable of getting on with things herself.

I did not see Lucy again, but I had an email from her some weeks later, asking if I could write her a reference for a college placement. I replied asking for more detail so I could shape my wording appropriately, but I never had a reply. Another student told me that she was working in a shop in town, but this was unconfirmed. Some months later, the school told me that Lucy had left home and was living in a flat with a friend and had secured an apprenticeship.

I often think of Lucy and wonder how she is doing. I know deep down that she is probably doing really well. The professional in me wishes Lucy all the best and thanks her for the journey we shared together. The real me wishes Lucy all those things but still holds out a small hope that she thinks of me sometimes too.

PETER

Peter had been referred to me following a safeguarding incident where he had been reported as having a same sex relationship with an older boy. At the time Peter was 15 and the boy was 17. The pair were reported by a Church leader who had been told in confidence about their relationship but had taken the decision that the matter should be investigated.

Peter had taken the news badly and had told a friend that he had considered suicide. He had been taken straight to a GP by his mother and the GP had determined that the suicide risk was low and that he was happy for Peter to return to the safety and support of his family. The family had reported the matter to the school and a referral had been made to me.

As Peter entered the room, he was extremely nervous and quiet. He was tall and very slim; his hair was almost too dark for his white complexion. Peter sat down and began to crack his knuckles.

"How are you Peter?"
"I'm very well thank you, how are you?"
"I'm well, thank you for asking. What brings you here?"

Peter reminded me of a character from an old Hollywood movie. His mannerisms were old fashioned, and his voice and dialect were like an Oxford schoolboy from the 1950's. I liked Peter straight away.

"Well, things seem to have been overshadowed by this safeguarding nonsense. My Mother and the school seem to think I'm in imminent danger of killing myself or falling prey to a sexual predator, but everyone seems to rather be missing the point. You see, I'm broken hearted" Peter spoke with such eloquence that I had to pull myself back into the room to focus on what he had said. I felt that I had just listened to the opening paragraph of an audio book.

"Tell me how things are for you then Peter"

"Difficult. As you have probably guessed, I'm gay, which, in itself makes things more difficult. Add to this my age…15 and his age…17 and you seem to have a melting pot of iniquity at the deepest level. All they seem to care about is my age and I dread to think what is going through their minds. Nothing sexual happened we just fell in love."

"You say it's difficult, but it seems it's difficult for other people rather than yourself"
"Yes, I suppose I am. They think it's difficult but that then impacts on me because they make it difficult for me. Do you see?"

"Yes, I see. It feels like they are focussing on what has happened but from your point of view maybe they haven't really stopped to think about you in all of this?"

"Yes, you could say that. Not that I want them to dwell on me too much, that would be ghastly! It's just that they don't understand"

Peter had gone on to tell me about his friendship with Aaron the other young man. Both keen members of the Church Choir, they had spent a lot of time together practicing and putting together performances.

Peter was particularly talented and had been nominated for a scholarship at a Public-School specialising in fostering talent such as his. Peter also had a talent for producing excellent performances and when he wasn't doing so for the Church Choir, he spent many hours helping the school's performing arts students with their productions.

Peter was openly gay and was accepted by all who knew him for being himself. By this I mean that Peter was regarded as eccentric by those who knew him and anyone who was asked about him would say "He's just Peter" Peter was also an A Star student and had been predicted a clean sweep at GCSE.

There was one family member, however, who didn't share Peter's World. Peter's father was an angry and resentful man. He had separated from Peter's mother some years previously and had always been a difficult person within the family, making the smallest of arrangements into major incidents. Peter told me that his father was an intellectually brilliant man, perhaps verging on being a genius. He had successfully created a career in astrophysics and was internationally eminent in his field. He had worked with NASA and had produced some life changing pieces of research. Peter wasn't entirely sure what had happened to his father, but he had heard family whispers that a research paper had been rejected as nonsense by the world of astrophysics. Unable to deal with the conflict of ideas, Peter's father had given up everything and now lived in a rented flat which was barely navigable due to the thousands of books and junk he now piled up around him.

"He thinks I'm a useless puff" stated Peter
"And what does that feel like?"

"Well, I know I'm a puff, but I try to hope that I'm not entirely useless" A wry smile came across Peter's face, but I knew that there was more to this. I couldn't help but make a link between the brilliance of Peter's father and his own talent although in very different fields and I wanted to investigate more how Peter felt about his own success. This would have to wait, however, as Peter was keen to talk more about Aaron.

"I could talk to Aaron about it and he, well, he just, understood you see" Peter and Aaron's friendship had developed with their shared love of debate and they often talked into the small hours about all sorts of topics.

"One night we were talking, and I asked Aaron if he wanted to watch a film, we had both been discussing earlier. We sat next to each other on the sofa and the energy between us was electric. I wasn't even watching the film as I was so absorbed in this magical feeling." Peter paused and looked up at the ceiling wistfully. "Our hands edged closer and closer until our little fingers were touching. It was like a gorgeous electric shock. At that moment, I felt like I had been transported to another World. I didn't understand what was happening"

As Peter told his beautiful story, I felt that I had been swept into his World and without realising it, I had again become his spectator. Like any good book or film, I found myself dying to know what happened next.

"We looked into each other's eyes and no words were needed. We leaned forward and kissed, it seemed to both last forever and be over in a split second. We watched the rest of the film in each other's arms and I smiled for the whole evening" I wanted to show my appreciation of the love story and my pleasure with the outcome by giving a burst of applause but, luckily, I retained enough wherewithal to simply say…

"That's beautiful Peter, thank you for sharing it with me"
"Why wouldn't I? How could anyone think that such a thing was dirty or wrong? I don't understand why it's not allowed. I'm six-

teen next month so if the news had been told a few weeks later, none of this would have happened"

I understood Peter's frustration as did the school and his mother who had asked for no further action to be taken. Even at 15, Peter was far more mature than many adults and after all, nothing had happened. Peter had not been coerced in any way into kissing Aaron, far from it; they had entered into the kiss consensually.

Whilst School were happy to take no formal action except for referring Peter to me, the Church had not been so lenient on either Peter or Aaron. Peter did not know what had been said to Aaron, but he had disappeared both physically and virtually with no trace of him anywhere on social media. Peter had heard that Aaron had moved to Manchester and that he had a new boyfriend. Peter meanwhile had had all his freedom taken away by the Church. He was always to be chaperoned when in their care and would have to speak to one of the Church appointed Counsellors. These talks, Peter had reflected, were little more than bible sermons preaching the evils of distractions of the flesh and any physical desire was something to be controlled and stamped out. All eyes were on him as he went about his business in the Church and he was regarded either as a defenceless boy, taken advantage of or as the work of the devil himself.

What I found strange about Peter was that none of this seemed to bother him in the slightest except for it being a source of mild amusement. What did seem to bother him and baffle him, however, was that Aaron had moved away and moved on, seemingly disregarding Peter and what they had. The way that Peter navigated his feelings around this and even the way he told me that he had become so frustrated that he wanted to commit suicide got me thinking.

Peter displayed many behaviour traits that I would credit to Asperger's Syndrome. Some would say that each and every one of us sits somewhere on the spectrum that ranges from serious problems functioning in society to people seeming slightly strange or finding others strange and incomprehensible in their behaviour. Many people who display the traits of Asperger's Syndrome will most likely struggle with emotions, especially subtle emotions as they simply don't see the World in the way that we do. Sarcasm, gentle facial expressions, even words used which mean something other than their literal interpretation can be difficult for someone with Asperger's to cope with. People who feature on the Asperger's spectrum may well enjoy indulging in complicated and passionate conversations about a chosen topic which may seem odd or irrelevant to us. For example, Peter knew everything there was to know about the Church organ. He understood the pipe work and how different sounds could be made. He was able to distinguish between tunes played with certain pipes open or closed and could name several organ designers along with their birth and death dates and any other incidental information about them.

Peter had not seemed upset about his father's behaviour towards him as to Peter there was logic in his comments. Once Peter got onto a subject, it was invariably very difficult to move forward with him without being somewhat abrupt. Here I should also explain that what we would term as abrupt, i.e. "Peter you have to stop talking about organs now as we need to move on" when he seemed so happy in his verbal dance; is merely a logical request and Peter would normally stop immediately and ask me what else I needed to talk to him about.

Peter had no time for friendships if they didn't serve him, as he couldn't understand the way they worked, nor did he want to. Once he had made a connection, however, he was fiercely committed to that person or project. This helped to explain Peter's struggle with Aaron. He had made a connection to Aaron and it was strong. It had been reciprocated by Aaron which, as far as Peter was concerned was the cement he needed. Peter simply couldn't see why Aaron had left him. Trying to explain how Aaron must have felt or been made to feel was very difficult. Peter refused to accept that there was any wrongdoing in their relationship (I was inclined to agree) and therefore, Aaron should still be here, by his side.

Peter had obtained Aaron's number, how I had not asked; and was now in some dialogue with him. I advised Peter that this was not necessarily the best idea as things can get misconstrued when texting, but he seemed intent on getting some answers from Aaron.

At our final meeting before the Christmas break, Peter had seemed agitated throughout. As he was preparing to leave, I asked him if there was anything else bothering him as he seemed distracted. "Well, I wasn't going to say anything but it's just not right for me to ignore it"

I wondered what the problem could be. With a little over a week to go until Christmas Day, I selfishly hoped that it was nothing too serious. "Go on"

"Well, it's your jumper"

"My jumper?" I looked down at my red jumper which was emblazoned with a white reindeer. "Do you like it?"

"It's not a question of whether I like it or not, truth be known I'm indifferent to it. What bothers me is that it's a Christmas Jumper"

"Yes?"

"It's not Christmas"

"But it's Christmas *time*"

"Strictly speaking Christmas or Christmastide begins on 25th December and lasts for 12 days following that. It is therefore not Christmas time or tide for another 10 days. You should therefore not be wearing that jumper. Enjoy your holiday and I'll see you soon."

Peter left my room and I stared open mouthed at him. I chuckled to myself and shook my head. Peter's refreshing honesty made me like him even more, even though I'm sure his only feeling for me, much like his feelings for my jumper was indifference.

2

We had taken a break in our work together over Christmas and I was preparing to return to School for the New Year. The School had forwarded an email to me from Peter who had requested an urgent meeting with me upon my return.

"Dear Sarah,

I respectfully request that I can meet with you at your earliest convenience in the New Year. There has been some movement in my situation over the break and I feel I should speak with you.

Regards,
Peter"

At Peter's request, I added him to the top of my list for my first day back at work. I asked the student support team if they had any information other than the email and they had heard nothing. "No news is good news!" quipped Lynn, one of the student support team.
Peter arrived a few minutes early for his appointment. I asked him to come in. He was pensive and moved slowly.

"How are you Peter?"

"I'm not at all well in every sense of the word" Peter had a heavy cold and his white skin was even paler against his black hair and red nose.

"Oh dear, I understand that you were keen to see me to talk about some stuff that happened over the break"

"Yes, it was pretty horrendous"

"When you're ready, tell me about it" Peter blew his nose noisily and closed his eyes whilst he composed himself.

"As you know, I had been in contact with Aaron and this continued over the holiday. Things seemed to be going well. We were talking and Aaron told me that he felt bad about leaving but he had been given little choice by the Church who intimated that he may be charged as some sort of paedophile. Aaron said that things weren't going well with his new boyfriend and that he was unhappy. He told me that he is coming back to the area for a recital at the local Church in a couple of weeks, but we mustn't meet or be seen together at all. This brought all of those feelings back again. The nice ones but also the horrible ones about him leaving me. I couldn't cope with them and had no idea what to do. I was in the Church at rehearsals and my chaperone had to take a telephone call. I seized the opportunity and ran and hid. I don't even know why, I just wanted to hide in a small place where no one could talk to me. The Church is massive so easy to hide in. I felt like my head was going to explode and I wanted it to. I wanted to explode and not have to have these feelings anymore.

When they found me, they asked me why I had hidden away, and I told them. Before I knew it, they were taking me to the car and they drove me directly to my GP, calling my mother en route. They told the GP receptionist that I required an emergency appointment as I was suicidal. I didn't understand how they thought this from what I had told them."

What Peter was describing to me is very common in people of

all ages who are dealing with trauma. In Peter's case, the trauma was, in part, due to his Asperger's Syndrome which diminished his ability to cope with strong feelings or to understand why once again Aaron was "leaving" him. It is of paramount importance when dealing with anyone who expresses a desire to harm or kill themselves that their intention is explored. It was clear to me, as it had been to Peter; that his intention was not to kill himself, he simply wanted the noise in his head to stop. The Church staff had panicked and taken immediate action which caused Peter even more distress.

"I became panicked in the surgery and tried to run away, they ended up restraining me and literally carrying me by my two arms and two legs like a demented superman through to the Doctor. By this time, I was having a panic attack. Thank god, the Doctor threw them all out. It was like a scene from a bad cop reality show" I was glad to see that Peter's dry sense of humour had not been affected. I smiled in support of him.
"Peter this sounds truly awful, I'm so sorry that you had to go through this"

"The Doctor was pretty good to be fair, I calmed down and we talked. I told him the same story and he confirmed that I wasn't suicidal at all, but it might help me to talk to someone about how I'm feeling. I told him I had you and he seemed fine with this. He told me to try and speak with you as soon as possible, hence my email"

"Well I'm glad that you feel comfortable to tell me all of this, how are you feeling now that you've recounted the story out loud?"

"Much better. It really helps to just talk, I never thought it would, but it does."

"I do have to ask, however, given the circumstances, whether you are or have at all been feeling like you may wish to harm yourself since the incident"

"No" Peter's confidence in his answer and also his inability to lie were enough for me. "Mind you, I might need some help with refraining from killing those idiots at the Church! They have me on some sort of suicide watch! I'm not even allowed to pee on my own now"

"I'm sure they're just trying to do the right thing for you, but I admit, it seems a bit heavy handed"

"Oh well, I guess I'll just have to deal with it, maybe I'll pretend I have a weak bladder and have them accompanying me to the loo every five minutes"

"And how is your mom doing? It must have been scary for her to get a call like that?"

"Well, here's the thing, my mom works for the Ministry of Defence in the HR department but as you can imagine, the security is extremely high. She's not allowed her mobile phone in the office so anyone who needs to contact her must go through the switchboard. All calls are screened, and a reason has to be given for the call. Can you imagine? *"Erm, can we speak to Mrs. Hayward please, it's about her Son Peter. Yes, he's just tried to kill himself"*

It's not the sort of call you get every day is it? She was having kittens by the time she arrived at the GP which would have been an hour's drive for her. Yes, I think she's ok, I didn't really ask her" My natural instinct to scold Peter for not asking or being interested in his mother was superseded by my theory about his Asperger's. Why would it occur to him that there may have been a problem?

It suddenly occurred to me that the Church was a large part of Peter's life and had a large influence on him. I wondered if it was totally imposed on him by them or whether he saw more of a link.

"Peter, you are very close to the Church, how do you feel about it?"

"I just love the pomp and ceremony of Church. The robes, the candles and the music. It's all truly beautiful don't you think?" I had to agree that regardless of my religious views, he had a point. Churches are often steeped in history and are one of the few institutions left where historical routine is observed. Cue one of Peter's in-depth monologues about the history of the Church, using words that I had never heard before let alone understood. Peter spoke like an eminent historian and I felt like an uneducated plebe in his presence. As it was nearing the end of the session, I decided to let Peter continue, partly because I didn't want to raise the subject of Aaron so near the end of our time and partly because I was more than a little bit entranced.

As we made our way through the New Year, Peter talked a lot about Aaron and how his head felt consumed by Aaron. He wasn't able to share his feelings with anyone else and communications with Aaron had all but ceased. Gradually, Peter was able to come to terms with the end of his relationship with Aaron and, perhaps conveniently for Peter, his GCSE's took precedence in the fight for his attention. I mistakenly felt glad for the distraction for Peter, but this was not to be the case. Peter had been formally accepted at the prestigious public school providing he met his predicted grades.

In GCSE year, students are tested over and over and sit previous papers regularly in every subject to help them prepare for the final exam. Usually, in the New Year, students will sit mock exams under exam conditions to give them a taste of what to expect. The exams are marked in house but using the criteria for the real thing. I often find myself explaining to students that they will not necessarily get the marks they expect because they are sitting an exam paper in January which contains content, they may not have learned yet. Alternatively, it's a chance for them to see any gaps in knowledge when they still have time to do something about it.

One of the issues that people with Asperger's Syndrome can be affected by is very rigid thinking. It can be very hard to convince someone with Asperger's that they are not entirely correct. Peter was no different.

Peter had been nervous leading up to the mock exams and had studied hard despite his natural talent. Peter couldn't even contemplate his life if he didn't make it to his new school. He was convinced he would be set free to live a life he wanted and enjoyed without ridicule or judgment, amongst people who were like him. I largely agreed as I thought that the new school would be full of "Peters" amazingly talented young people who had possibly suffered a life of torment. I shared Peter's excitement at this prospect but to Peter it meant much more and there really was no other option for him.

The Head Teacher had contacted me to say that following a weekend stay at the school and some informal auditions, Peter's acceptance at the school was now unconditional. Peter and his mother had been informed and she hoped that this might take the pressure from Peter.

When Peter came to see me that week, he was the most agitated I had seen him, even more so than when he had seen my Christmas Jumper.

"Hi Peter, is everything ok?" There are two chairs in my room. One opposite me, around two meters from me and the other, in the corner of the room is a spare chair. Peter went and sat in the spare chair, staring at the wall opposite and avoiding any contact with me.

I left Peter in silence for a while to allow him to settle in the room and gather his thoughts as I didn't want him to leave in this state. Peter sat slumped in his chair sulking with his arms crossed in front of him. His complexion was even more sallow than usual, even grubby looking and his hair was greasy, the kind of greasy hair becomes after several days of not washing.

"Have you finished your Mocks?"

"Yep"

"When do you get your results?" Peter reluctantly pulled his bag from the floor beside him onto his lap. He unzipped the bag and brought out a white piece of paper which looked like it had been screwed up and then opened and re folded. Peter reached out towards me, the paper in his hand. I opened the paper which was his exam results and started to read...
English A*, Maths A, Physics A, History A*, Chemistry A, Biology A, ICT A, French A*, Drama A*, Music B, RE A*

"Wow Peter this is amazing! Well done" As I spoke, I knew what he was thinking and what was coming.

"That's it, I'm done for. Failed, my whole life is ruined. They'll never take me now. Of all the subjects to fail it had to be Music!"

"A B is hardly a fail Peter; many students would be jumping for joy if these were their results"

"Well I'm not many students!"

"Have you spoken to your music teacher?"

"Yes, he says that I should have safely secured an A* but felt that I hadn't revised enough" I thought carefully before asking my next question.

"Could it be possible that you didn't revise music as much because you felt it was your strongest subject?" I winced inwardly waiting for Peter's reply.

"Er, well, now that you mention it; I actually didn't do any revision for Music. Why would I need to?" I waited in silence whilst Peter thought this through. "Mmm, perhaps I should have done a bit" I left Peter with his thoughts about his exams.

The next time I saw Peter we talked about his mock exam results. He told me that he had decided to erase the incident from his mind as to dwell on his failure was just too much for him to bear. Peter accepted my help to design a revision timetable and together we plotted times for him to revise all of his subjects. As study leave drew near, Peter and I talked about possible support at his new school. He told me that he would quite like to take me with him and put me in a room somewhere in case he needed to talk to me. I felt the back of my throat tighten and I twisted my mouth to disguise my chin wobble. I was touched, perhaps even more so knowing that Peter would not have had the same experience of counselling as someone without Asperger's Syndrome. It felt nice for me to realise that he had made his version of a connection with me.

I told Peter that I had learned a lot from working with him and thanked him for sharing part of his life journey with me. Peter looked at me in puzzlement. "What do you mean?" I smiled inwardly and decided to generalise my comment to help Peter understand.

"I always feel that I learn something from my clients, and I feel thankful that they trust me enough to talk to me about intimate feelings"

"Oh. Anyway, I won't see you again as exam study begins next week so I'll be at home studying or doing my exams, so, bye then"

Peter stood up and left just like that. I thought about our time together for quite a while afterwards and always had fond memories of Peter.

I talked to my Clinical Supervisor about how I felt about Peter and how much affection I had for him. This helped me to process my thoughts and to look logically at our journey and its inevitable end.

Fourteen months later I received an email from Peter. He apologised for not getting in touch sooner and had meant to contact me within his first year at his new school. Peter told me that the school was everything he had hoped it would be and more and he thanked me for helping him with his little "blip". Peter wished me and my family well and signed off.

He'll never know how much receiving that email meant to me, in fact, he'll probably feel indifferent about it.

OLIVIA

Olivia was different from a lot of girls her age that I had previously worked with. What struck me was her maturity. When we first met, Olivia was in Year 9, making her 13 which I found myself checking with her as she could easily have passed as 15 or 16. Olivia was referred to me because she had been experiencing some issues with her father.

As Olivia walked into my room, I noticed not only her physical maturity but her extreme beauty. Her father was British, and her Mother was Italian. Olivia was petite and curvy; her waist length brown hair was thick and shiny. As she sat down, she shifted the weight of her hair over her shoulder to reveal her engaging green eyes and full ruby red lips. With not a stitch of makeup, she reminded me of a young Sophia Loren. Olivia sat down and crossed her legs.

"Hi there Olivia, I'm Sarah"

"Hello, thank you for seeing me" as I went through the mandatory introduction and information, Olivia listened intently, nodding and remaining silent. Once I

had finished, I addressed Olivia.

Sarah Terry

"So, Olivia, how can I help today?"

"Well, it's kind of embarrassing really, I'm not sure it constitutes a need for Counselling, and I know there are plenty of others who go through far worse but it's just my Dad"

"Ok, what about your Dad?"

"Well, he sort of, well not *actually* but kind of, er hit, well not hit, that's wrong, he well he assaulted me" As openers go, this was pretty extreme. Of course, I had to remind Olivia that I would have to report the incident to Safeguarding colleagues and she was aware of this and happy for me to do so.

"Ok, so now we've got the formalities out of the way, do you want to talk to me about what happened?"

Olivia went on to tell me that she had been out for the day in London with her family who consisted of her Mother and her younger Sister, Lydia. She told me that her Dad had a temper anyway and her mother and sister "knew how to handle him". Olivia said that they knew when to shut up and so, she thought, did she.

"I hadn't even said anything, in fact my Sister was whining about something or other as usual and I think I told her to shut up. He just turned on me. Before I knew what had happened, he had his hand around my throat and pushed me up against the wall. My legs were dangling, and I thought he was going to punch me. A passer-by called over to ask what the effing hell he was doing, and he dropped me and stormed off."

"Olivia that must have been awful and really scary. Can you remember how you felt at the time?"

"Erm, I wasn't really scared as such, I was just thinking what a dick head and what an idiot you must look, holding a 13-year-old girl up a wall by her neck"

"Ok, so how were your Mom and Sister?"

"Same as usual. They just carried on as if nothing had happened and then we all went for a meal" I felt myself filling with rage inside, but this would not serve Olivia.

"Olivia, do you realise that this is not normal behaviour? I don't just mean your Dad but also your Mom?"

"Yeh, I know" said Olivia with a half-smile. "But it's how my family reacts so I have to deal with it" she shrugged her shoulders.

"Has this happened before Olivia?"

"Not as bad as that, I think that was the worst he's ever been, but he shouts all the time and throws and slams things around. The only person who seems to get through to him is my Grandma. She and I are really close, and she understands him better than my Mom."

Olivia seemed to gain momentum and went on to tell me that her friends were scared to come around when he was there, and they had all commented that they felt he treated Olivia unfairly and differently from Lydia. Olivia's dad seemed to take pleasure in putting her down and stopping her from going out or having any freedom. Olivia's mother, in her words was next to useless and the family dynamic resulted in Olivia spending most of her time in her room, alone.

She was not a fan of gossip over social media and so had not indulged in the usual group chats and snap chats that most of her friends lived for. This had made her somewhat a target for ridicule which although it annoyed her, I couldn't help thinking that she courted it also. She told me about an ex-boyfriend who seemed to take great pleasure in calling her names and generally being a pain in the back side. Olivia often felt that she had no one to talk to and she felt sad and alone a lot.

"I know I can't change things and I'm not bothered about that but it really helps to just talk through with someone how I feel knowing that my confidence won't be betrayed like it has with others" Olivia had told her ex-boyfriend about her father and the way he was and he now found it funny to tell anyone who would listen that "Olivia is such a skank that even her own Dad hates her!"

"And what is that like for you?" I was trying to get an idea of what made Olivia tick. She was strong and intelligent both academically and emotionally, I could understand how this might enrage her father and her lack of reaction to him would probably help to fuel his behaviour. In fact, it could easily be misconstrued as goading him.

"It's just annoying really. I just can't wait to get out of this school and then hopefully go to Uni and start my own life" I found myself agreeing with Olivia internally that this would be a good bet for her.

Our first session went by in what seemed like a nano second and I was interested in finding out more. I had to attend to the safeguarding issue and informed Olivia that I would be reporting it immediately. "Yeh, that's fine" she said.

"Moving forward Olivia, how do you feel about coming to see me again? Have you found it helpful?"

"Yes, I really have, thank you. It's nice to just talk to someone without having to worry." As I made an appointment with Olivia for the following week, I found myself intrigued and looking forward to it.

I went straight to the Head of Safeguarding and completed a safeguarding concern sheet. I was shocked to find that the incident had already been reported and seemingly dealt with. I was told that Olivia's parents had contacted the school to say that Olivia may say something. They had put the matter down to a family argument which involved Olivia's father having to restrain her by her shoulder and in the struggle his hand had slipped to her neck. Upon realising, he had immediately let go and felt genuinely sorry and remorseful for his actions. Mmmm...one to watch, I felt.

I did some work with Olivia about how she might come across to others. What she perceived as ignoring people and trying to stay out of trouble, may even be working in the opposite way for her. We talked about how she may come across as aloof and standoffish which certainly wasn't the Olivia I got to know. I found her to be funny, kind, thoughtful and interesting. She had a flare for writing and was writing about her life whilst we were working together. Olivia reported to me each week that she had tried new ways of interacting with people which despite being hard for her had shown positive results.

We had also addressed Olivia's relationship with her father which remained somewhat rocky. He worked away from home a lot so it was difficult for Olivia to try new things or spend time with him as he would only come back at the weekend which would usually be packed full of social engagements. One idea that Olivia had come up with was to pretend that she was doing a project at school where she had to research some information about her parents. She had asked her father and surprisingly, he had agreed. He suggested they go to her Grandma's as she would be able to remember details of his childhood also. Olivia had been astonished to find that her father had been thrown out of school when he was 14 and had to fend for himself. He now had a very successful business which afforded them a very privileged lifestyle, but he never forgot where he came from and how close he became to never having a decent life. Both he and Grandma told Olivia that she reminded them so much of him, her headstrong ways, refusing to conform and not responding to authority. Olivia's dad feared that she would end up the same way when he had high hopes for her.

This was a great breakthrough which helped Olivia (and, I have to say, me) to see her dad in a different light. I talked to Olivia about the importance of walking in another's shoes and trying to imagine what it would be like to be them and she got this. She realised that her dad, although inappropriate in his execution had a reason for being so tough on her. It almost made her feel special.

I suggested that Olivia take the conversation further by acknowledging how proud she was of her dad and that she felt proud to be like him. She could take opportunity to remind him, however, that she *wasn't* him, she was her own person and she was a long way from being kicked out of school, she was actually excelling and so maybe she could take the family talent to a whole new level.

Olivia continued to report that things were better with Dad. He even asked her if she wanted to go and price a job up with him and they went for tea and cake afterwards. I had noticed that Olivia's cool exterior had warmed which served to radiate her beauty even more. Families like Olivia's rarely end up happy due to the personalities involved and sure enough as Olivia's relationship with her Dad grew, her relationship with her mother declined.

2

We were approaching the end of May holiday week and Olivia's family were due to go abroad for the week. Olivia told me that she had been trying to lose weight even though she didn't want to. Olivia was far from skinny, but she was also far from fat. She was curvy, which doesn't seem to be a realistic option in the early 21st Century. Her mother, who she told me was very slim, even anorexic; according to Olivia; had told Olivia that she was fat and that she would be embarrassing them in a bikini in her state. I shuddered. Olivia went on to tell me that she had no desire to lose weight as she was quite happy with the way she looked but she just went along with it to keep her mother happy.

"What's she gonna do? Leave me at home?" Olivia laughed, "Maybe I'll eat a bit more on the sly and put on weight, that'll teach her" Once again, Olivia seemed refreshingly unperturbed by the comments from her mother and very self-assured and self-aware. The more I got to know her, the more I realised that she was becoming quite a remarkable person and all the things that were wrong in her life were teaching her and serving her well.

Olivia told me some heart-breaking stories and some hilarious stories which urged me to think that her memoirs will be a best seller. She told me that her sister, Lydia had been sent to a private school locally. Olivia had not been given the option, but her mother had told her friends that it was because Olivia was not clever enough. Lydia, who adored Olivia had been in trouble almost every week since she had been at the new school and wanted to attend Olivia's Comprehensive. Her compliant nature at home was clearly fuelling her behaviour when she was free of her parents. Olivia was often dragged along to hockey matches, ballet classes' tea parties etc. where the mothers of Lydia's peers would look her up and down disapprovingly and remark, "Is this the other sister? The one who didn't get in?" Olivia would laugh at them and think them stupid.

Olivia lived in a very large house out in the country and so was often isolated from her friends. Her mother, on the other hand, had made great efforts to become one of the gang. She had champagne get togethers, where her friends would arrive looking like an advert for Harper's Bazaar and slag everyone they knew off. Olivia would take great delight in coming downstairs in her onesie and slippers, eating; only to giggle when her mother ushered her upstairs against the backdrop of the disgusted expressions of her friends. Olivia joked that her mother thought she was in an episode of a TV reality show about rich housewives and Olivia was the disrespectful, difficult child.

Olivia was often left waiting at the school gates when her mother had either been too busy or had forgotten to collect her. Olivia would simply say, "I wish she had told me, I could've got the bus with my friends"

Olivia was not allowed out at the weekend unless she had a lift from her mom or dad. Mom was always too busy, and Dad was rarely at home these days, even at weekends. Mom had decided that Olivia should have some more suitable friends and had set up meetings with her friends and their daughters, all of whom shared the same look of mild disgust. Olivia found them vacuous and boring, they barely acknowledged her.

Olivia's confidence was high, and she felt she fitted in at school a little more. She could put up with her mother and, apart from wishing she was leaving school, all was well. It was coming up to the main summer holidays at school, so Olivia and I decided to close. I reminded Olivia as I do with all students that they can come back to see me any time if things change and she went on her way.

3

It wasn't until mid-way through the following year that Olivia requested to see me. She had started to wear makeup which, being Olivia, she had obviously thought through and wore well. Her pale olive skin was covered in a dewy foundation and her cheeks were gently highlighted with a pearlized hue. Her plump cheeks were dusted with a rosy blush which accentuated her cheekbones. She had expertly drawn wings over her eyelashes which opened her green eyes even more together with a brush of mascara. Nude lip gloss finished her look and her hair which was still naturally coloured fell around her face.

Olivia greeted me with a big smile and sat down. "How are you Olivia?"

"Mmmm ok I suppose"

"Talk to me"

"Well I seem to have a little trouble with an ex. I suppose you could say he's been stalking me" Once again Olivia seemed to have drawn attention to herself in a way which seemed out of sync with her personality.

Olivia had been dating this young man for a few weeks, he was from a different school and a different area. She had also become close with his mother and, for a while things seemed to be working out. As time went on, Olivia began to feel that her boyfriend and his mother were very intense. "They would include me in family discussions, arguments and even when they argued, they would both ask my opinion. I quickly learned that this was a dangerous game as a couple of times, I ended up being the bad guy. I decided to finish with him and that's when it all started. He was all over my social media so I blocked him from everything but he is friends with some of my friends on social media so he could look at what I was doing and comment. Then, worst of all, his mom got involved and he started slagging me off saying I was disgusting and had hurt him deeply, so much so that he had contemplated suicide. It's all pretty heavy stuff really."

"Olivia, I have to tell you that this is a safeguarding issue and I have to report it as I feel that you could be in danger here."

"Well, I told my Mom and Dad and Dad replied to one of his posts saying that if he continued to harass me, they would call the police. Things seem to calm down after that, so we'll see."

"Ok, I'm glad you told Mom and Dad and that Dad has done something about it. I'll still have to log the incident here though and make a note that parents are aware, is that ok?"

"Yes, no problem"

"So how has this whole thing affected you?" In my mind I was thinking that things seemed to have moved on at home by the way that Olivia was talking about her parents. I wanted to ask her about this but now wasn't the time.

"I just feel a bit crap really. You know, sad I suppose"

"Tell me why you feel that way"

"I dunno really it's just that I feel how I did before, you know, just a bit down in the dumps" Olivia had realised that she had drifted from some of her friends at school but her best friend who she had confided in on a few occasions had been telling other people Olivia's secrets and this had led to some rude and offensive comments being made to Olivia. "They're calling me a slag and saying that I've done things, sexual things and I haven't. I had a couple of experiences with my ex but nothing like they are saying. It just feels like I'm in the spotlight again and I don't like it." Once again, I found myself feeling puzzled about how Olivia was feeling and how she may have unwittingly brought about the situation. I decided to broach this with her.

"Olivia, it seems to me that for someone who is very independent and has worked on and been through some of the things you've been through, drama seems to be around you quite a lot. How do you feel about it?" Olivia laughed.

"You're right you know, I thought this myself. I have a funny story, totally unrelated to what's going on. I went to my sister's school nativity play with my mother. Of course, all of her posh friends were there, and she had her eyes on me like a hawk. I was trying to fade into the background and my mother gave me the job of taking some photos. It was really hard to see so I crept around the side of the audience and crouched down to get some pictures only to be told off by one of the teachers. I got up to walk back to my seat and saw my mother scowling at me. Before I knew what was happening, I felt myself tripping over a cable. It turned out to be the electric cable for the humongous Christmas Tree!" By this time, engrossed in Olivia's story, I had my hand to my mouth with my eyes wide open dreading what she would say next. Olivia was laughing herself by this point. "Don't worry, the tree didn't actually fall down. It swayed quite a bit and a few baubles fell on the floor. In the panic, a few of them fell to the ground and some of the parents jumped up from their seats. One of the Dads fell backwards and knocked over the manger." By now, Olivia was struggling to talk as she was laughing too much and I was laughing with her. "And…and th…oh…and then, Baby Jesus fell out of the manger and…" Olivia had to pause to compose herself for a moment,

"His head fell off!" We both screamed with laughter. Olivia was crying and so was I.

When we had calmed down, I asked Olivia how she had felt at the time.

"Horrified! It was like everything happened in slow motion. I just stood there and when Jesus had been safely returned to his manger, all eyes switched to me. I looked around the room and felt my mother's eyes boring into me. I couldn't look at her." Olivia was still laughing. She went on to tell me that her mother hadn't spoken to her for a week after the incident.

"And what was that like? Surely she realised it was an accident?"

"Yes, but it embarrassed her and that's worse than cold blooded murder in her eyes."

"You don't seem upset?"

"I'm not really, I'm used to it to be fair, I'd rather be me than my little sister. Being the disappointment is easier than the one they all pin their hopes on. I find they tend to leave me alone and now I'm a bit older, they let me out to meet friends. If anything, they probably prefer that as I'm out the way, so everyone is a lot happier these days"

"So, tell me more about how you are feeling though. I'm confused because on one hand things seem to be better at home and you seem a lot happier but on the other, you say that you are feeling sad again?"

"I don't know really, it's just that I get this way sometimes and I can't explain it. It's like it comes from nowhere and I can't seem to get over it"

"Ok, have you noticed a particular time when it happens more?"

"Not really, it just sort of creeps up on me"

"It's possible Olivia that even though you seem to be able to shrug a lot of things off, things with your parents and such, they are actually negative things that are still happening to you. Do you understand what I mean?"

"Er I think so. I never really thought about it like that. I suppose I'm so used to coping with stuff that it doesn't seem like an option to not be coping. it's a bit embarrassing really"

"Why would you think that it's embarrassing?"

"Well, you know, a bit, weak. Getting upset coz, your parents have a go at you sometimes"

"First of all, Olivia, what you have described to me about your life and some of the things you have been through is far from normal. I work with lots of young people and what you talk to me about is a form of abuse. Just because your parents provide a wealthy lifestyle and you have nice things doesn't mean that you are immune to abuse."

"I wouldn't go so far as to say I'm abused though, there are people who suffer far worse than I do"

"Suffering is all about perception. What is suffering to one person is everyday life to another. We should never underestimate the damage that our lives can do to us if we leave ourselves unchecked and choose to ignore the warning signals" Olivia went quiet and seemed deep in thought. "How do you feel right now Olivia?"

"I don't really know. Weird"

"What I'd like you to do is take some time when you are alone to really think about what is making you feel sad. When you get the sinking feeling in your tummy, I want you to acknowledge it and talk to it." Olivia looked puzzled. "Bear with me, I'm not suggesting you walk around having a chat with yourself, this might look a little strange. I want you to use some visualization techniques here. Now, being a writer and a creative person, I'm guessing that you use your visualization skills often without even realising it. I want you to make a visualization for the feeling. Can you do that for me now?" Olivia paused for a while and shifted in her chair. She looked up at the ceiling for a few moments and then closed her eyes.

"Dread! A Black shadowy figure whose name is Dread" Olivia seemed pleased with herself.

"Ok, let's have a chat with your friend Dread. First, you need to understand that you created him for a reason and that reason was probably to help you to do or not do something." Olivia was excited and eager to speak.

"Yes! He helps me to stay in a safe zone, out of trouble if you like."

"Ok so what is the dread for you?"

"That I'll do something wrong"

"And what would happen then?"

"Mum and Dad would be even more angry" I noticed that Olivia had adopted childlike mannerisms as if she were recalling a younger version of herself. "If I do what he says, he'll be able to look after me. He's my friend"

"Ok, brilliant. So, we've acknowledged that Dread is your friend and the feeling that you get when he is around is the sadness that you talk about. Is that correct?"

"Yes, it's as if he's reminding me that he's there and that I need to behave so he can still look after me"

"Ok, I wonder if you don't always want him to look after you? Maybe now you're older you can decide how to behave and if he comes to you it's your choice whether you listen to him or not. He can still be your friend and maybe your friendship can change a little bit, much like it does with your friends at school"

This had been a breakthrough meeting for Olivia, I could see the relief on her face. When Olivia arrived for her next session, she had her journal with her. She had dedicated a whole chapter of her book to her friend and had decided that he had a new role. She had explained to him that from now on, his job was going to be to help her to be herself and if she made a mistake, she could talk to him and together they would see how they could change things for next time. She had also decided that since he was her friend, it didn't make sense for her to feel bad when he was around, so she now felt comforted and happy when he came.

It had also answered a lot of questions for me about how Olivia had courted attention and yet felt uncomfortable with it. Her unique personality was pushing through but the coping mechanism she had developed as a child was no longer needed. Olivia did indeed have the confidence to do anything she wanted, she also had the maturity to see her parents for who they were and accept them without blaming herself for their inadequacies. Olivia was a big personality bursting with gifts which I deeply hoped she would go on to share with the World.

FLISS AND JACK

I like to think of Fliss and Jack as my Bonny and Clyde. Two characters who individually had their issues but once they came together the madness, anger, fear and passion were squared. They had set themselves onto a collision course which no one could stop or help them to foresee.

Fliss had been working with me for a year or so since Year 11 when she was 15. She had been a difficult girl for the school to work with and although she would dodge lessons and tell teachers to Fuck off, somehow; everyone saw the vulnerability in her and chose to see past the bravado. Nonetheless, her constant rule breaking, and non-attendance had to be dealt with and Fliss was heading for permanent exclusion which would greatly reduce her chances of taking her GCSE's. As usual, I was seen as a last resort attempt to try and get Fliss to open up and help her to see the importance of taking her exams.

The Inclusion manager, Lina had approached me and asked for some help. Lina had excellent relationships with her students and often invested her own time in dealing with some of the more challenging ones. Fliss, however, had taken exception to Lina and would not cooperate with her at all.

"Please Sarah, you have to help me with this one. She's intelligent and more than capable of passing her exams but she's a bloody nightmare! She won't cooperate, she won't even bloody speak to me! She hates me and I can take that, but I don't hate her, and I want her to do well even if it's so she can stick two fingers up at me!" Lina and I laughed. So often when we are working with vulnerable teenagers, they become aggressive because it's the only thing they know how to do. They try to share their anger and despair by being rude to us or refusing to do as they are asked. We understand it and we deal with it because we know it's not personal and we don't take it personally. If it makes them feel better to think they have upset us, we let it go until they learn that we keep coming back to try and help. At this point, the most aggressive and out of control teenagers will become a compliant friend for life who, maybe for the first time in their life are able to let go and trust an adult. That's when the real work can begin.

I had met Fliss a couple of times when she was speaking to Lina and she had been in Lina's office after leaving or being thrown out of class. She was a very pretty girl with small, sharp features, high cheekbones and a softly freckled nose which gave way to milky skin and peach lips. Her face seemed almost too small to house her doll-like eyes which were black brown with the longest thickest natural lashes I have ever seen. There was a real sadness about Fliss, and I often struggled to see how she could be rude and aggressive when her voice was mostly barely audible. I had made my peace with her when she had been lurking in reception one day after an argument with Lina, threatening to walk out of school. Sue, the school receptionist was trying hard to keep Fliss in the building by offering to make her a cup of tea. She was becoming increasingly flustered as Fliss refused to acknowledge her. I emerged from my room which was based within the reception area and Sue looked at me helplessly, flashing her eyes towards Fliss. I had managed to coax Fliss into my room where I was able to talk to her and find out what had gone on. It struck me how quietly she spoke and anything I could hear was barely a mumble. It was the same old story, a teacher had asked her to remove her coat and she had refused, leading to her being exited from the classroom but protesting her innocence and unfair treatment. I had allowed Fliss to calm down and talked to her about how angry she was and what might be causing it. To my surprise, she had opened up and told me about some problems at home between her parents and how this was affecting the family as a whole. I had listened and allowed Fliss to talk and she seemed to calm down. As she left my room, she thanked me for listening.

Ever since then, Fliss had acknowledged me politely so Lina thought it was worth giving things a go. Fliss had questioned what I would be able to do. She correctly pointed out that I couldn't solve the problems between her and her mum and dad and since that was her main concern it seemed pointless talking to me. Even so, Fliss agreed to give it a try.

Our first meeting was awkward. Fliss sat across from me and barely made eye contact. She sighed a lot and played with the plastic curly telephone cord, rolling it between her fingers. I allowed Fliss to stay quiet for a while and after a few sighs I asked her if there was anything she wanted to talk about. "There's nothing you can do anyway" she mumbled, "It's nice that you want to help and all that but what's done is done"

"I'm curious to know what you mean when you say that Fliss. I don't have any background to your family story except what you told me when you came into my room a couple of weeks ago. Are you happy to tell me a bit more?" Fliss shrugged her shoulders.

"What's the point? They're kicking me out of here anyway and my mum's kicking me out too so I've got nowhere to go, I may as well just become invisible"

"Ok, you say you think the school will kick you out, I get where you're coming from as I know you're on a final warning but what about your mum, what do you mean that she'll kick you out?"

"She doesn't want us, any of us but it's ok for my brother and sister as they're Dad's but I'm not so he won't want me"

"Your Dad won't want you? You say you're not his, but you call him Dad?"

"Ok, Stepdad then"

Fliss had told me that her mum had been in two previous relationships. Once with the father of her two older siblings, who now had families of their own and saw their dad regularly and again with Fliss's dad who had turned out to be a drug addict who had beaten Fliss's mum. She had fled him and brought Fliss with her and there had been no contact since. Fliss's mum often told her that she assumed that her father was dead due to the lifestyle he had led.

Fliss's mother had met her stepdad and had gone on to have two more children. A boy aged 10 and a girl aged 8. The five of them had lived happily until the marriage began to break down and things went from bad to worse. Fliss, by her own admission had been difficult at the time and had regularly argued with her mum. Once her stepdad had left the family home, Fliss would regularly stay with him and sometimes for longer periods of time when arguments had been worse.

It also transpired that Fliss's mum had spent periods of time in residential mental health facilities. Fliss wasn't sure but felt that there may have been some ongoing mental health issues with her mum although this didn't stop her from being angry with her mum and feeling abandoned by her. Even armed with this knowledge, it was easy for me to see why Fliss would be angry and what might cause her irrational behaviour. There was more to come however, lots more.

I often thought of Fliss as a helpless feather blowing in the wind, rather like the seeded head of a dandelion whose direction is dictated by anything or anyone other than itself. Its delicate white-headed stems blown for miles not knowing where or if it will land safely and be able to complete its journey. Sometimes, the head may be picked up or blown away several times before it finds a place to root. Fliss clearly had not found that place to root and felt at the mercy of all around her, grabbing desperately to anything over which she had the remotest of control. Currently, she had found that she could control her environment at school by misbehaving. Her reward was a guaranteed outcome which she could predict and attention of which she had none.

Fliss seemed to have resigned herself to her life and would often tell me that she didn't care about anything as what was the point?

Fliss's family were also receiving help from Social Services as her younger siblings' teacher had flagged that there seemed to be some changes in their behaviour and had also noticed an irrational array of adults collecting the children. When their mother had refused to come into school to talk to the head teacher, the school had gone over her head and referred the family to social services. Fliss's mother had been difficult to engage but her stepdad had been happy to finally receive some support and advice.

The support worker who had been assigned to the family asked to meet with me when she had visited the school to see Fliss. Fliss had refused to talk to her saying that she would only talk to me but had nevertheless been happy for the support worker to tell me what had gone on so far. Apparently, Fliss's mother had not attended any of the meetings and was not replying to requests for contact. Fliss's stepdad had asked if he was able to have Fliss live with him as she was not his biologically, but he wanted her to come as she was to all intents and purposes his daughter. I was pleased to hear this. The support worker went on to tell me that Fliss's stepdad was a nice guy and wanted to get everything sorted for the kids, but her mother was making life very difficult. I asked the support worker if there had been any mention of Fliss's mothers' mental health issues and there had been. Luckily, social services would have the power if necessary, to intervene if things became impossible to sort out.

2

I continued to see Fliss for several weeks and for a long time, things didn't really change. She was now living with her step-dad but still had issues around her confidence in him and that he really wanted her to live with him. Fliss would constantly tell me that he only took her in because he had to and if he had the choice he would not have. I reminded her every time she mentioned it that he in fact did have a choice and he had chosen for Fliss to live with him. Fliss's mother came in and out of her life, demanding to see her one week and ignoring her the next. Gradually, Fliss talked less and less about her worries about her mother and stepdad and more about normal family stuff. Her demeanour improved and she was not getting into trouble so much.

It was our last session before Christmas and Fliss was eager to see me. When I got to school, she had left a message at reception to ask if I could see her first today. I had to attend a meeting with the Head Teacher first thing which ran over a little. When I came out, Sue was waving a piece of paper at me from her seat in reception. "Don't tell me…Fliss!" I said as I made my way towards Sue.

"She's been down twice to see if you're hear. I think she might explode if she has to wait any longer. I've written down where she is, and she's asked us to send for her as soon as you're free"

"Ok then, let's see what's so important it can't wait!"

Fliss practically burst into my room that day. "At last! You're here. I've been waiting to tell you"

"Tell me what? I can't wait any longer, the suspense is killing me" Fliss had been predicted good grades even though she had missed a lot of learning, but these had dipped recently as the lack of attendance had taken its toll on her. Fliss had been disappointed to hear that her latest predicted grades for GCSE were C's and D's. This is where I began to see a new side to Fliss. Far from sitting down and taking what life had thrown her way, Fliss came out fighting. No longer a dandelion in the wind, Fliss was as solid as a rock and was carving her own future.

"There was no way I was walking out of here with crap grades, it's just not happening. So, I've decided to do something about it" Fliss was like a child telling her mother that she had achieved something. She was exceptionally keen to let me know that she had sorted everything out. She had been to see all of her teachers and had asked to attend extra lessons and revision sessions and had also asked if she could take old exam papers home to complete and would they mark them for her. Some of her teachers had been understandably dubious but she told me that she had asked them to give her one more chance and had agreed a time limit of two weeks. If she wasn't putting the work in, they could withdraw their support.

I was dumbfounded. I had always seen that Fliss had a spark inside her which she had been expressing as anger, but she had really turned things around for herself and was showing maturity beyond her years.

Fliss returned to school in the new year with the same attitude and was working really hard. She stayed behind almost every night working and attending revision sessions. She seemed a lot happier in herself and had even attended an interview to join the school 6th Form. She had been offered a place providing her grades and her attendance were satisfactory. Fliss had something to work for and something to aim for she was even looking forward to attending her school prom.

For this period of time, our sessions largely comprised of Fliss telling me how well she was doing both at home and at school. Her stepdad had met a new lady friend and Fliss liked her. Life was good. Until one day in February.

3

Fliss's birthday was coming up and she was excited about getting a new laptop from her stepdad and a new phone from her mum. She had told me that she had chosen what she wanted and couldn't wait to get them.

It was the week before Fliss's birthday when she came to see me. She had been crying and was very quiet. Her voice had returned to the almost inaudible mumbling she had displayed when we first met.

"I hate my life, everything's just crap what's the point?"

"Well Fliss, this seems like a turnaround from before. Things were going so well, what's happened?"

"No one cares about me; I knew it wouldn't last"

"Tell me what hasn't lasted Fliss"

"My mum of course, she wants nothing to do with me...*again*"

"Your mum wants nothing to do with you?"

"She hates me and doesn't want to see me, she told me to forget my birthday present and to forget her as I won't see her again" I felt I had to qualify what Fliss was saying. I knew her mother had a history of erratic behaviour, but I never thought she could stoop so low as to cut her daughter out of her life, especially the week before her birthday.

"So Fliss, sorry to sound like I'm not getting it, but you say that your mum doesn't want any more to do with you? Is this just you or your brother and sister as well?"

"Nope. Just me" Fliss slumped back in her chair and started to pick at her nails. I left her in silence for a while to see if she would elaborate. After a minute or so, Fliss looked up at me through her endless lashes. She raised an eyebrow as if to question me. I didn't respond. Fliss stretched her arms out in front of her, her hands interlinked and yawned.

"I'm so tired, I only had about an hour's sleep last night" Fliss completed her stretch and looked at me with renewed vigour. "How was your weekend anyway?" There was a strong sarcastic tone to her voice.

"Not as eventful as yours it would seem" I raised an eyebrow back at Fliss, letting her know that I wasn't going to let the conversation end there. Fliss smirked and rolled her eyes knowingly.

"What do you want to know?"

"Er…everything?"

Fliss pulled her phone out of her bag and began searching through her messages. She seemed to scroll the screen forever looking through reams of text.

"It's easier if I just read it to you" Fliss went on to read the conversation between her and her mother which still left me dumbfounded. The premise was that Fliss's mother hadn't been able to afford the phone she wanted after all and had told her so. Fliss had said that this was ok, and she understood but could she still have a new phone even if it wasn't the expensive one she'd chosen. Fliss's mother at this point launched into a personal verbal attack of Fliss, saying that she was ungrateful, only caring about herself and she only wanted a relationship with her mother so she could get things. Fliss had always been the same and she should wonder why anyone bothers with her. Fliss had tried to respond by saying that she didn't care about the phone and it was ok if she didn't have anything to which her mother had responded that Fliss was lying and she knew that she did care really and it was best that she break off contact. With that, Fliss's mother had proceeded to block her from all social media. Fliss had been told by her friend that her mother had taken to Facebook to post messages saying that children were ungrateful and whatever she did, they didn't really care about her and were generally shitty people. When people had asked what had happened, Fliss's mother had named her and told them that she was basically a bad person.

Fliss flopped back in her chair and threw her phone on the table. "There you go, that's what my mother thinks of me" As a mother myself, the one thing that I never seem to be able to get used to is parents who don't seem to care about their kids. They put themselves first and genuinely have no regard for the consequences. I really didn't know what to say to Fliss. I knew what I wanted to say. I wanted to tell her that her mother was a bitch who ought to know better and she seemed so self-absorbed that she hadn't stopped for one minute to think how Fliss would feel. I knew however that whatever I thought of Fliss's mother, Fliss loved her and always sought her approval and love, which annoyed me even more. Part of me also suspected that within a few days, the roller coaster would have completed its journey, and all would be well again between Fliss and her mother.

Sure enough, the following week, Fliss reported that things had been settled with her mother who had also bought her the phone she originally wanted. I wondered how a young person with a life as hectic and unpredictable as Fliss's could function. Somehow, Fliss not only functioned but seemed to excel. As each week went by, her confidence and her grades improved, I hoped each week that there wouldn't be any more drama for her to contend with. Luckily, for these few weeks, there wasn't.

The time came for Fliss to be released for her study leave and she was reluctant to go. She did attend several revision sessions and popped in to see me from time to time. Things were going well, and she felt ready for her exams. She had chosen her Prom Dress which her mother had insisted on paying for and even had a date for the evening. In a flash, Fliss was coming to tell me that she had just completed her last exam and that things seemed to have gone well. I wished her all the very best for the future, and she was gone.

I felt apprehensive for Fliss. I felt that she needed the achievement of her GCSE's going well and I worried that a negative outcome may hit her hard. All was in the hands of fate and of course Fliss.

I received two emails that summer from Lina, the first was a picture of Fliss at her Prom looking stunning in a rust coloured silk dress which hugged her tiny frame and complemented her colouring. The flash of dark red lipstick she wore was all she needed as somehow it seemed to make her naked face look like she was fully made up, enhancing her piercing black eyes against her pale skin. Fliss was laughing recklessly in the picture and had asked Lina to send it to me so that I could see her dress. It was a beautiful picture in many ways.

The second email I received was from Lina which again Fliss had asked her to send on to me. It was Fliss's results. She had secured all 11 of her GCSE's scoring B's and C's across all subjects and had been accepted to the 6th Form. Fliss had asked if she could still work with me and Lina had agreed that yes, she could.

The Fliss I saw when we returned from the summer break was very different. I had only ever seen Fliss in a school uniform or a prom dress and had no pre-conceptions about her personal style. Fliss's mid back length hair had been cut into a sharp bob which swung just above her shoulders. Her shiny brown hair was kissed with golden highlights. Fliss's skin remained make up free and the only addition she had made was a brush of black mascara which she barely needed.

Sarah Terry

I was pleasantly surprised to see that Fliss's personal style was quite tom boyish. She was wearing baggy jeans which she had rolled to just above her ankles to reveal black socks and docker style shoes. Fliss wore a baggy brown top which on many girls would have looked somewhat dowdy. On her however, it only served to enhance her colouring. More than Fliss's clothing though, I noticed that she had lost quite a lot of weight. Her previously normal frame was now very slim indeed and her tiny face took on even more of an elfin appearance. Fliss walked in and sat down.

"Do you think I've lost weight? Everyone keeps telling me I've lost weight. I think I'm fat though" Alarm bells rang for me as Fliss had never before mentioned that her weight was a problem. In these situations, I am always careful not to get drawn into giving an opinion as it's important to decipher what is going on for the young person.

"Do *you* think you've lost weight?"

"Not really" Fliss stood up and examined herself "I've been eating, well, when I say eating, I mean drinking" She laughed.

"So, you've been partying, have you? Well-deserved I'd say. Well done on your exam results Fliss you smashed it and by the way you looked stunning in your prom dress too"

"Thank you, yes I'm really happy with everything and thank you for your support, I couldn't have done it without you."

"Nonsense Fliss, you did all the hard work and it paid off for you. Anyway, how is life treating you at the moment?"

"Not too bad really, Dad and his new girlfriend are spending lots of time together which is nice. It's also nice to have her around as Dad is happier and we get fed too"

Fliss went on to tell me that she was expecting her new timetable later that day and was excited about seeing her new lessons. She had been to numerous parties over the summer and had really enjoyed letting her hair down. I reminded her that there was more hard work to come and she laughed and told me she had it covered.

Something inside me doubted that Fliss was going to have an easy time but I believed in her and hoped with all my heart that she would make it. Time would tell.

4

Jack was referred to me following an outburst in lessons where he became angry and verbally abusive towards his teacher. Jack's mother had been called into school to discuss the matter as the outburst seemed to be totally out of character. The school had offered my services and Jack and his mother had been keen to take them up on it.

Jack was a small very slim young man who had dark features borne from his mixed-race background. His mother was white British whilst his father was Armenian. Jack had jet back wiry hair which he wore close cut. His skin was dark olive and his big brown eyes were set deep into his small face. Jack was in 6th Form but had the physique of a much younger boy, I would have gone so far as to say that his body looked pre-pubescent. Jack probably stood no taller than 5'3 or 5'4 and his skinny jeans fell baggily around his legs. He looked like he had raided his older brother's wardrobe.

On our first meeting, Jack had refused to sit down and had paced around my room for the first half of our session. He seemed very agitated and was teary eyed as he talked about his relationship with his mother and his father who were now divorced. Jack had witnessed his father's domestic violence against his mother.

Jack's father had never been physically abusive to him but was constantly verbally abusive. Jack now lived with his mother and stepfather and saw his father occasionally. Jack had a very rocky relationship with his mother, who; it turns out was also verbally abusive towards him. She was exceptionally controlling and had access to his phone records, monitoring his every move. She would ensure that she reminded Jack every day of how useless he was and how, if it weren't for her, he would be heading for a disastrous life of poverty and crime just like his father. Jack's father, on the other hand had taken to nurturing from afar and congratulated him for "surviving life with that bitch" Jack's father blamed his mother for the domestic violence and his angry behaviour towards Jack. Jack was torn between the horror that he remembered such as when he had seen his father slap his mother and spit in her face or when he had seen his father press his mother's hand onto and electric cooker element; and what his father was telling him. After all, Jack had witnessed his mother's less than acceptable behaviour towards himself and had felt first-hand the anger which built up inside making him want to hit her.

Jack was shaking at this point as he paced back and forth, tears in his eyes and his fists clenched. "I just don't want to become him! What if I hit her and then that means I'm like him" At this point, Jack's own words echoed through his head and it was too much for him to bear. He began to sob uncontrollably; his face was crimson, and he held his hands up to it to try and hide it. I silently opened a packet of tissues and handed him one. He snatched the tissue from me and turned his back on me. He blew his nose and dabbed his eyes. "Sorry, God I'm so sorry that was really embarrassing"

"Please don't feel embarrassed Jack. I actually see it as a good thing that you got upset. It's usually a good way of releasing feelings. How are you feeling?"

"Actually, better thank you" sniffed Jack. I handed him another tissue and he sat down to face me. "Sorry, I bet I've ruined your day"

"What makes you say that?"

"Well, the last thing you want is some kid coming into your room getting upset and chatting shit about his dysfunctional family" I said nothing and smiled at Jack, waiting for him to process what he had just said. "Oh wait, that's your job!" We both laughed and the tension had been broken.

I guessed that it was very difficult for Jack to talk to me and, as I suspected that I was probably not dissimilar in age to his mother; there was probably an extra barrier for him to overcome.

"Jack, I feel your frustration and from what you have told me so far I can see where it comes from. It sounds like you're in a pretty difficult situation and I can see that. You have two parents who I'm sure love you, but it seems that they have been confusing you with their behaviour. You feel that you don't want to be violent like your father but on the other hand you seem to have no voice with your mother, and you are unable to let her know how you feel. The frustration builds up and the only solution you've seen in your life is violence both verbal and physical. The good news is that you recognise it and the fact that you are angry about it means that you don't want to resort to these patterns of behaviour." Jack looked at me silently for a few seconds.

"But what if I can't stop myself? What if I lose it with her or someone else?"

"Have you done that so far?"

"No"

"What's the most extreme behaviour you've ever displayed when you've been angry or frustrated?" Jack thought for a while.

"Erm, I dunno"

"What do you normally do when you're angry?"

"I just walk away and go to my room if I can"

"So, what happened with your teacher the other day? Presumably you couldn't get away to another room then?"

"No, I felt trapped and she kept shouting at me to sit down. I just wanted her to shut up, so I told her to fuck off and leave me alone. She told me to get out and that's when I could escape"

"And when you get away, what do you do?"

"I just sit and try and calm down. I breathe deeply coz I read somewhere that helps"

"And does it?"

"Yeh, I suppose it does"

"Brilliant! So, what we *can* say is that you are at least one step ahead of your parents. You are managing your anger. Do you see that?"

"No. I never looked at it like that before, it's just what I do"

"Ok, well I want you to start and look at it differently. I want you to be aware of what you are doing and re label it as managing your anger." Jack smiled.

"Cool! I like that"

Jack and I only had a few sessions together and he seemed to move on really quickly. I suspected that he would have more work to do as he matured but he had experienced the support of being able to talk to someone and it had been a positive time for him. Jack asked if he could stop seeing me after our fourth session as he felt so much better. As the work I do with students is voluntary,

I agreed, giving Jack, the option of returning should he feel the need.

5

Some weeks went by and Fliss seemed to be getting on with life and getting into her studies. Our sessions were mostly to update me on that she was doing and which parties she had attended. She had expressed a mild concern that she should slow down on the partying and maybe pick up a little on the studying. Overall Fliss seemed happy and much more capable of coping with her family problems. Fliss's mother continued to pick her up and put her down when it suited but Fliss seemed to have come to terms with this. She seemed in a happier place and was making new friends.

Fliss had mentioned a friend called Jack a few times but I did not make any connection, after all, it's a popular name. It was another new year and Fliss was preparing for her first set of Mock Exams before taking her first year A level exams in May/June.

Fliss had made a New Year's Resolution to quit drinking and partying in place of studying which I felt was very sensible. Her friend Jack was helping her, and they were study partners. They encouraged each other and supported each other through the mock exams.

Fliss did fairly well in her mock exams and was told by her teachers that she was well on track. I wondered why she didn't seem happy though.

"Fliss that's brilliant news and all down to your hard work. I bet you feel a sense of relief now?" Fliss shrugged her shoulders.

"S'pose"

"Oh. Well that wasn't what I was expecting, what's up?"

"Aah it's not me, I'm fine, pleased actually. It's Jack. He cocked it all up and failed everything"

"Oh no what a shame, I know you both worked really hard to revise together."

"Yeh, well, they're saying that he might get kicked out if he doesn't make the grades. I've told them that if he goes, I go"

"Oh, Ok, that's quite a big reaction Fliss. Tell me more"

"Well he's the only one who's ever been there for me when everyone else turned their back on me, Jack was there. He never judges me he just supports me"

"That sounds like a really important relationship Fliss. Tell me why you feel Jack is the only one who ever supported you."

"Well you should know more than anyone what I've been through, so I don't really see why you're asking me" I was taken aback by Fliss's reaction. I would tread more carefully when talking about Jack and what he meant to her in future.

"Yes, I understand Fliss and it's horrible to watch someone you care about suffering."

"Yes, it is. I can't bear to see him so unhappy and if it means I have to give up everything to be with him and look after him then that's what I'll do" I decided to resist the instinct to talk to Fliss about how throwing away her future as well would not serve either of them. I could tell that she was in no mood to hear anything but praise for Jack, so I decided a total change of direction was needed.

"So, Fliss, you haven't really told me much about you and Jack so far. I know you're study partners and great friends so tell me all about him" Fliss smiled embarrassingly and began to fiddle with a pen on the desk.

"Have you guessed yet?" She gushed "You know, that he's my boyfriend?" Of course, I had suspected some time ago but Fliss for whatever reason had not wanted to divulge. I sensed she wanted to shock or surprise me with the news, so I obliged.

"No! Really? Well you kept that one quiet!" Fliss giggled and her mood instantly lifted.

Fliss told me all about Jack and how, since meeting him she was a changed person. She no longer drank alcohol as Jack didn't see the point and they rarely went out with other people as they preferred to keep themselves to themselves. Fliss told me that Jack understood her because he had experienced problems with his own family. "In fact, you know him! When I told him about you, he said he had been to see you last year. You helped him with his anger management and how to handle his mum" I tried not to give a reaction either way but as Jack had told Fliss that he had been to see me, I had to admit it.

"Well I shouldn't really be telling you but as you already know, it seems I did see a Jack and it sounds like the same Jack. As you know though Fliss, even that is more than I can say"

"Oh, Yeh I know but we tell each other everything anyway"

Inside my head was an alarm bell which was ringing out so loud it made my ears buzz.

The next week when I arrived at school, Sue, the receptionist had a note for me. "Could you please see the Head of 6th Form today? She wants a chat with you. It's about Fliss and Jack" I raised an eyebrow and Sue mirrored me. "I don't think it's good news. Shall I call her and tell her you're here?"

"Yes, please Sue, we may as well get this over and done with" A few moments later, Angela Gould, the Head of 6th Form knocked my door. She was a tall imposing woman who was slim but thick set. She reminded me of a shot putter or a judo fighter. Her face was very stern, and her blotchy red skin clashed with her over bleached white chin length hair. She met my smile with a blank expression and I almost felt as if I were in some kind of trouble. Without any introduction or verbal greeting she barked.

"You have to sort out this situation between Fliss and Jack. It's just a joke. Neither of them are applying themselves to study and they're swanning around the place missing loads of lessons. I've spoken to them both and warned them that if they don't sort themselves out, they'll both be leaving 6th Form. I simply can't have this disruption" When she had finished talking, Angela Gould; still standing, folded her arms and tapped her left foot. Her face had become even more red and blotchy and her blank expression was now verging on a scowl. I was aware that I had pushed myself back into my chair and I felt quite intimidated. At this moment, I felt sorry for any students who had to encounter her wrath.

I often work with teaching staff and try and have a blended approach for students where possible, but I had taken exception to the manner in which Angela Gould had ordered me to do something about Fliss and Jack. What did she expect me to do?

"Ok, well it's nice to finally meet you Angela" I couldn't resist. "So, there seems to be a problem with Fliss and Jack. I'm not sure I can help"

"Well they both seem to think you're the best thing since sliced bread, so I assumed you'd be able to do something. You're obviously doing something we're not so that's why I came to you" This woman was trying my patience and her sarcastic tone, I felt, implied that she thought that I may think I'm in some way better than her and her staff. I couldn't help thinking that if her approach with students was anything like this, I wasn't surprised she didn't get anywhere.

"Well, thanks for letting me know there's a problem. Have you told Fliss and Jack that you're speaking to me?"

"Yes"

"Ok well, I'm seeing Fliss today, but Jack is no longer on my list."

"As of today, he is" At that moment, her phone started to buzz. "I need to take this" and as abruptly and rudely as she had entered, Angela Gould left my room.

"Bye then" I whispered after her. I took a couple of deep breaths to cool down and compose myself and I had to walk around for a while, so I left my room and walked along the corridor the short distance to reception where Sue was looking at me knowingly.

"Lovely isn't she" quipped Sue and we both laughed.

When the time for Fliss's appointment came, she was visibly agitated. She sat down abruptly and threw her bag on the floor. "Are you ok Fliss?"

"No!" Fliss sat silently for a few seconds and then she began, "Who the fuck does Mrs Gould think she is? She's a nasty cow, I hate her. She won't leave me and Jack alone. Jack doesn't need to come and see you, in fact he can't, I've told him, it's wrong. I know I haven't got a say in it, but I can't see you while he sees you. I just can't, he can't it's wrong. Well what I'm saying is, if he needs to see you, he can but I won't" Fliss folded her arms and sunk down in her chair, scowling.

"Well as you probably now know, Mrs Gould has asked me to see Jack today to talk about what is going on with you and him. She tells me that you're skipping lessons and obviously you can't really afford to do that. We just want the best for you and…" Before I could finish my sentence Fliss interrupted me.

"It's got nothing to do with that though. There aren't any problems as such, it's just that Jack hates some of his lessons and I feel bad for him being on his own."

"But Fliss, that's not good. You're doing so well, and this time is so important. If Jack is struggling maybe, we can talk to him, but you must concentrate on yourself" I could hear my motherly concern spilling over into lecturing Fliss, but I felt compelled to try and help her to understand. It was too late, I had crossed the line and in so doing, became another nagging voice. Fliss stood up purposefully and grabbed her bag from the floor.

"D'you know what, forget it. Just forget everything it's all a load of crap anyway." Fliss flounced out of my room.

I knew I needed to let her calm down and I also felt her frustration at the possibility of Jack seeing me and talking about things that she may not be happy for him to share. I would have this conversation with both of them and re-iterate my rules around confidentiality. If it came to it, I would have to speak to the lovely Mrs Gould about a conflict of interest for Fliss. As it happened, this would not be necessary.

Jack came to see me at lunchtime to tell me that he would not be seeing me as Mrs Gould had wanted and he had told her so. He didn't feel that talking to me would help him and he wanted to leave 6th form anyway. He hated his subjects and his teachers, and the school were crap. He also said that he had spoken to Fliss about her leaving also so that they could attend another school or college together. He thanked me for my concern and left.

It was the end of the school day and I had heard nothing from Fliss. I was writing up some notes and gleefully setting out an email to Mrs Gould, telling her about what Jack had said. There was a gentle tap at my door. "Come in" Fliss peered slowly around the door. "Hi Fliss, come in" I motioned for her to take a seat.

"Are you sure? Bet you hate me"

"Of course, I don't. You were angry and I didn't really help. Shall we draw a line under it and start again?"

"I'm really sorry."

"So am I, let's move on"

Fliss was all too aware of Jack's visit to me which I guessed had been manipulated by her. She felt happier that Jack had refused to see me. My curiosity about their relationship and how it might affect them both, however, would have to wait for another day.

The next time I saw Fliss, she told me that Jack had left school to start an apprenticeship. She seemed relieved and I took my opportunity to dig a little deeper.

"How do you feel about that Fliss?"

"Dunno really, pleased for Jack I s'pose. He's a lot happier which means everything is calmer as well."

"Everything is calmer, what do you mean?"

"He gets, you know, a bit, well hyper when things aren't going his way and he tends to take it out on people closest to him, like me and his mum" I remained silent and waited for Fliss to expand. "He can be, well angry and aggressive, not physically y'know but with words. Like, he calls us names, like stupid bastard and stuff like that. It's ok though, I understand him. His mum thinks I'm brilliant with him. She says she doesn't know what she'd do if it wasn't for me"

"And how is that for you?"

"It's nice, she's like a mum y'know? She cares and she notices when I do things. His stepdad is really nice too. They make me feel at home so I don't mind it so much if Jack is being an idiot, I can take it"

"So, it's the sense of family that you are drawn to? And even though Jack can be difficult sometimes, you can put up with it because you feel at home with his parents?"

"Don't get me wrong, I love Jack but yeh, I guess it makes it easier. It's nice" Fliss sat back in her chair and rolled her scarf around her hands, she brought the scarf up to her mouth and smiled into it, her black eyes dancing at the thought of the acceptance she felt, and the slight embarrassment she had at telling me. Looking at her like this reminded me that she was indeed just a child and although she was strong, determined and feisty, she was also desperate for a mother's love.

I felt uneasy with the relationship between Fliss and Jack and his family. I could see that she would put up with almost anything if it meant she felt that she belonged. Fliss looked at me and it was as if she had read my mind. "I know what you're thinking, you think I'm silly and I'm only with Jack because I haven't got my own family and it makes me feel part of theirs. I guess it does, but I know what I'm doing" Fliss returned her scarf to her face and sat back in her chair, one eyebrow raised over her mischievous eyes, those eyes!

"I just want to explore with you what it is that you get from the relationship so that you feel comfortable in it as it seems to me that sometimes you don't"

"I'm ok…I am!" Fliss smiled at me as she both reassured and

warned me off in the same retort.

"Ok, let's leave it there then but I just want you to know you can talk to me about it anytime"

"I know, and I'm really grateful for that, truly"

Over the next few weeks, Fliss and Jack continued with their rollercoaster relationship, Fliss continually accepting and enabling Jack's worsening behaviour. He was struggling with his apprenticeship and was starting to skip days at college, expecting and encouraging Fliss to do the same. Fliss had bunked off a couple of times but, so far, was committed to staying in school. The price she had paid for this was the wrath of Jack who blamed her for his failure and constantly accused her of not caring about him and what he was going through.

I could see that the cycle of abuse was continuing, and Jack's behaviour was starting to concern me. I had decided that I was going to disclose my worries for Fliss's safety as a safeguarding concern and prepared myself to talk to Fliss about this in our next session.

Fliss was her usual self and reported to me a great weekend where she had been out for a meal with Jack and his family. She was happy and upbeat, and I knew this was going to be hard.

"Fliss, I want to discuss something with you which I'm not sure you're going to like much, but I have to say it" Fliss stopped her fidgeting and stared me straight in the eyes. Her black eyes narrowed, and she leaned forward.

"You're not leaving, are you?"

"No, I'm not leaving Fliss"

"Oh God, that's ok then, I thought you were going to tell me that you were leaving. Well, whatever you've got to say is ok then" As Fliss relaxed back into her chair, I sensed it was going to be very far from ok.

"Fliss. I have some concerns which have been troubling me for a while and I feel that out of concern for your personal safety, I need to share my concerns formally with the school" Fliss by now was staring at me, her ruby red lips framing her tiny wide-open mouth.

"What? Is this a joke?"

"No Fliss, it's not a joke"

"Well what do you mean concerns?"

"Fliss you've been telling me for some time that Jack has been verbally aggressive sometimes and…"

"Oh, come on, are you being serious right now? You think Jack would hit me?" I ignored Fliss's interruption and continued.

"And you have also mentioned that he can be controlling and blames you for his failings."

"Yeh, so? It doesn't mean he's gonna hurt me! Oh my God this is the most ridiculous thing I've ever heard! You're supposed to be the one person I can talk to and now you're doing this to me" Fliss gulped back her tears.

"Fliss I always said that if I had any safeguarding concerns, I would discuss them with you first and this is what I'm doing right now. I see a troubling pattern of behaviour with Jack; and you yourself have said it's getting worse. I must make sure that you are safe in case anything happens"

"So, what are you going to do?"

"I'm going to compile a safeguarding report which I will send to Lina Gill for review. Mrs Gill will then most likely want to chat to you and may want to discuss the issue with your parents"

"Oh well, that's just great isn't it! My mother doesn't give a shit and my dad has enough on his plate. He'll just have a go at Jack, and he'll say it's all my fault, except this time, it will be!" Fliss jumped up from her chair and gathered her bags together. "Thanks for nothing!" She slammed the door as she left. I never saw Fliss again.

7

I completed my report to Lina who followed it up with Fliss and her parents. Lina later told me that I had not been the first person to raise concerns about Fliss and Jack, but she had done all she could and had left the matter with parents.

Two years later I was contacted by police and asked for details of the work I had done with Jack. He had been arrested for a violent attack on his mother. She had been hospitalised and had agreed to press charges to help Jack get the help he needed. My stomach flipped when I heard the news. I wanted more than anything to find out if Fliss was still involved with Jack but of course the police were not able to divulge this information. Fliss had cut all contact with me when I had told her that I would be referring her to safeguarding. She told Lina that I had let her down and that I hadn't understood what she needed from me. She told Lina to tell me that I would never see her again.

I had visualised Fliss saying this, those back eyes flashing with golden venom, her tiny nose scrunched in anger. I had also reflected on how much my actions would have hurt her and how alone she would feel with no one to talk to.

There was nothing more for me to do, I had done my best and although I mourned the ending for Fliss and I, I could sleep well at night knowing I had done the right thing.

CONCLUSION

The word "conclusion" is, I feel, totally inappropriate. By definition it is an ending, a resume of what went before, closure. The stories here are far from complete. They are just at the beginning.

The experiences these young people have had will shape their futures and the futures of those around them. Their ripple effect may only reach a few generations, but it will go on to influence, good or bad, what comes after they have left this earth. And so, we have a responsibility to ensure that our own stories shape us in a way that will make us happy with our own legacy, from World Leader to prison inmate, we all leave a mark on our World.

I hope that each of these young people and the many more that have touched my life will find their own way. I'm sure they will and some of them, somewhere along their journeys; may give me a thought and be reminded that once, someone listened to them, without judgement or agenda wherever possible. And I also hope that this may give them the courage at a time in their lives when they need someone to listen because they just might have something life changing to say.

So, I want to thank the amazing young people who have changed my life for the better and taught me so much about facing adversity, being strong, being vulnerable, seeing and making progress. Being human.

Printed in Great Britain
by Amazon